BAD PETS
Most Wanted!

D0071752

BAD PETS
Most Wanted!

ALLAN ZULLO

Scholastic Inc.

To Maddie and Randy Manausa, with hopes that none of their pets will
ever do anything crazy enough to make it into another book like this.
— A.Z.

ISBN 978-0-545-67534-5

Copyright © 2014 by The Wordsellers, Inc.
All rights reserved. Published by Scholastic Inc.

SCHOLASTIC and associated logos are trademarks
and/or registered trademarks of Scholastic Inc.

12 11 10 9 8 7 6 5 4 3 2   14 15 16 17 18 19/0

Printed in the U.S.A.
First edition, September 2014

40

CONTENTS

WILD AND WACKY

There is no end to the outrageous, hilarious, and weird things that our pets and wild animals will do. Their capers and shenanigans leave their owners and victims shaking their heads in amusement, befuddlement, and yes, occasionally, anger. It's been that way forever.

Some of their craziest antics in recent years have been documented in *Bad Pets: True Tales of Misbehaving Animals*, *Bad Pets on the Loose!*, and *Bad Pets Save Christmas!*. But three books can't come close to covering all the animal kingdom's impishness and goofiness. So here is another lighthearted collection of true stories of animal mischief ranging from the absurd to the zany.

For example, you'll read about the dog that went for a joyride in his owner's car . . . the skunk that played a key role in a football team's defeat . . . the cat that kept stealing neighbors' underwear . . . the pet parrot that destroyed an expensive designer gown . . . the raccoon that stole purses and wallets from golfers . . . the seagull that swiped a video camera and recorded its crime . . . and more!

Whether they walk on two legs or four, have feathers or scales, live on land or in water, one thing is certain: Animals of all kinds can be wild and wacky.

THIEVES

ARRESTED DEVELOPMENT

Cato the husky was under house arrest after he was charged by police with shoplifting from a Dollar General store in Clinton, South Carolina.

The canine criminal usually enjoyed hanging around the house. But whenever he had the chance to slip away, he headed for downtown establishments. One December morning in 2013, Cato got off his leash and went looking for trouble.

He found it at the nearby Dollar General store. Surveillance video showed that the dog walked through the automatic doors and went right to the shelf that displayed dog treats. Cato helped himself to a little package of beef bones, trotted out the door, and buried his ill-gotten gains near a neighboring car wash.

A short while later, as the video revealed, he returned to the store, where he spent three minutes deciding what item to steal next. He chose a package of pig ears. Once again, he sneaked out of the store and buried the tasty booty.

The persistent thief wasn't through with his crime spree. When he entered a third time, Cato tried to swipe a box of dog food. But the canine got caught red-pawed before he could "flea" the scene. That's when store manager Anastasia Polson checked the store surveillance cameras and saw what he had done. After dropping the box, Cato was allowed to leave, and Polson discovered where he had buried the goods.

Even though the four-legged crook had been given a chance to go home, he tried to get back into the store again. "We had to lock the [automatic] door to keep him from coming back in," Polson told WHNS-TV.

Finally, the store manager summoned police, who arrived with an officer from the humane society and a dog catcher. Being the friendly dog that he was, Cato gave himself up without incident and was transported to the local animal shelter until his owner, Holly Darden, could be contacted.

"My dog is a shoplifter," she told WHNS. She said she didn't know why he would steal dog treats because she fed him well. "Look at him, he's fat," she said. Pointing to her kitchen, she said, "There's food in there. There're treats in there."

Although it was Cato's first "arrest," Darden said she wasn't sure if this was the dog's first theft because he had slipped into several downtown businesses before. Citing two grocery stores, she said, "He's gotten into Ingles. He's gotten into BI-LO. He goes to Pizza Hut."

Darden offered to pay for the stolen items from the Dollar General and promised to "cur"-tail her dog. Polson declined to press charges against Cato, giving the dog a new leash on life.

Oscar the dog didn't let his disability keep him from shoplifting. The ten-year-old, three-legged German shorthaired pointer brazenly ambled into a store and swiped some dog food. Then he tried to steal two more times before he was nabbed.

One day in 2013, the pilfering pooch followed customers into the Alray Dairy in Invercargill, New Zealand, and walked over to the open refrigerator section of the store. Despite missing his right back leg, he stood up on his good leg, stuck his face into the freezer bin, and surveyed the meats that were on display. He ignored the more expensive cold cuts. Instead, he set his sights on a packaged roll of meat made specifically for dogs. He picked it up with his teeth and then sauntered past startled customers and went out of the store without stopping at the checkout counter.

After patrons alerted store owner Esmay Hay, she viewed video of the theft on surveillance cameras. An employee searched for the dog without success, but did find evidence of the crime — a torn wrapper of the $5.40 meat roll that was about three blocks away.

Emboldened by his successful caper, Oscar returned a few days later, but was run off by a customer. Not easily deterred, the dog came back again. This time, employees were ready for him. When he entered the store, they captured him without a fuss.

Eventually, Oscar was turned over to the local dog pound, where John Youngson, city council manager of environmental health, learned that the pooch's owner was on vacation and had left him in the care of a relative. But because the relative didn't have a fence, Oscar was allowed to roam.

Apparently, the cunning canine had cased out the store before the theft, because outside surveillance cameras showed a dog that looked suspiciously like Oscar snooping around after the dairy had closed.

"He's not your usual shoplifter is he?" Hay told New Zealand's 3News. "No, they're usually of the two-legged kind."

She said she had no bone of contention with Oscar because, "You couldn't be angry with him." Hay refused to press charges, saying that if Oscar was brought to trial, "he wouldn't have a leg to stand on."

STRICTLY FOR THE BIRDS

On a lark, wild birds have been known to swoop down and snatch video cameras — while recording their crimes.

An eagle in Western Australia grabbed a camera, flew for miles while it was recording, and ended up making a selfie.

The motion-sensor camera had originally been placed at a gorge on the Margaret River in the remote Kimberley region in 2013 by aboriginal rangers who wanted to capture images of freshwater crocodiles. The camera, which was about four to six inches long and two inches wide, disappeared several days after it had been set up.

At first, the rangers figured the camera had fallen into the water. But months later, the camera was found near the Mary River, about 70 miles away from the scene of the crime, Gooniyandi ranger Roneil Skeen told the Australian Broadcasting Corporation (ABC).

When rangers examined the video, they were surprised and amused to discover the identity of the thief. The first of three 30-second clips released to the media shows the young eagle snaring the camera and flapping its wings. Later, after it deposits the camera on the ground, the eagle poses for a selfie, poking its beak into the camera lens.

"It was pretty amazing, because it's one of the first camera traps to ever get picked up," Skeen told the ABC. "They've had camera traps moved [by animals] before, but not taken off, like a flying camera, you know? It was pretty cool, [and] we were pretty shocked."

Since the theft, the rangers bolted down the camera so there would be no more bird's-eye views of similar thefts.

A year earlier, a seagull stole a small video camera right out of the hands of a French tourist who was shooting beach scenes in San Francisco. The bird's entire crime was captured on video shot by the thief.

The tourist, 26-year-old Nathalie Rollandin, was holding her miniature GoPro camera and recording the sunset at the Golden Gate Bridge from the popular Crissy Field walking path. Suddenly, out of nowhere, the winged culprit snatched the camera in its beak and flew away.

Reportedly, Rollandin ran after the thief, which took the camera on a short joyride over the water along San Francisco Bay. Nathalie stopped people on the beach and drew rather strange reactions when she asked if they had seen a seagull with a camera in its mouth. Eventually, she was able to recover the camera after the bird landed about a half mile away on a walkway next to the St. Francis Yacht Club and dropped the camera.

In the video that the seagull recorded, you hear Rollandin shout with alarm as the bird flies off with the camera, which then records the perpetrator's low-level flight to the yacht club. In the final shot that the bird took of itself, you see it fly off into the sunset. A few seconds later in the edited version, Rollandin runs up to the recovered camera, aims it at herself, and laughs.

She uploaded the video to YouTube and it went viral. On her page, she wrote, "A San Francisco sunset I will never forget!"

PAWS FOR CONCERN

A crafty bear with a taste for German food figured out how to Dumpster dive out of sight of a restaurant's outdoor security cameras — by stealing the large metal garbage bins.

In 2013, a large bear was seen in a Colorado Springs, Colorado, neighborhood, foraging in commercial garbage containers and tipping over residential trash cans for food. One of his favorite eating spots was outside the back door of a popular German eatery, the Edelweiss Restaurant, which kept several metal bins for garbage and trash.

The bruin figured out a clever way to avoid being videoed while feasting on the leftover food that was tossed into the wheeled garbage bins. He simply got on his hind legs, grabbed a bin with his front paws, and, while walking backward, rolled it about 50 feet into the parking lot and out of camera range. Next, he flipped over the container, which weighed about a half ton when full, and opened the lid. Then he helped himself to German leftovers.

When restaurant manager Dieter Schnakenberg found the large container on its side in the parking lot, he thought vandals had done it. "I saw the Dumpster dumped over, and we pulled up the [security] video, and sure enough it is a bear," he told KCNC-TV. "The big bear wanders over and just grabs hold of it and wheels it away." He said the bear passed by the recycling bin without showing any interest in ecology and went "right for the good stuff."

When the bear had his fill, he left. But he came back the next night and stole another garbage bin. Schnakenberg estimated the bear was more than six feet tall when standing on his hind legs.

After the staff chained the containers and secured the lids, there was no more trouble "bruin" because the bear had "bin" there and gone!

FELINE FILCHERS

Cats in England have been finding windows of opportunity — literally open ones — to steal things from neighbors.

A family cat nicknamed Denis the Menace has been swiping items since 2012 — and there's no effort to stop his pilfering ways.

That's because the cat burglar has turned himself into an international celebrity. In fact, he's become so notorious that he even has his own YouTube page, featuring video of him bringing his stolen booty home at night.

The two-year-old black-and-white feline, owned by Lesley Newman, of Luton, Bedfordshire, England, was a rescue kitten that the family had since he was six weeks old. After Denis had been neutered, Newman let him and the family's other cat, Eddie, out for the first time when they were six months old. Once Denis was allowed to go in and out of the cat door, he began his life of crime.

A week after the cat's newfound freedom, Newman noticed some strange clothes that didn't belong to her lying around the living room. A week later, Denis brought home a Barbie doll.

"He either leaves things in the front room or brings them up to me in bed," Newman told the British Broadcasting Corporation (BBC). "He will come to my side of the bed and scream until I acknowledge what he has brought in. It's like, 'Hello, I've brought you a present.' In the past week alone, Denis has brought home a sock, towel, facecloth, glove, and a motorcycle crash helmet bag."

The list of items he's stolen is impressive. His haul includes shirts, underwear, an expensive polo shirt, a cardigan sweater, shoes, sandals, a pair of slippers, dozens of socks, tea towels, paintbrushes, a dog chew, toys, car wash sponges, gloves, and a soccer ball.

"He has completely filled two large boxes," Newman told Metro.co.uk in 2013. "I would say he has taken well over one hundred things now. He obviously thinks all these items are prey."

Denis has a particular fondness for stealing men's underwear. "He doesn't take briefs — only boxers," she told the BBC.

One night, he showed up with a woman's sandal that he had filched from a nearby garden. Then he went back a week later and returned with its mate.

"I tracked down the lady who lost her sandals," Newman told the *Daily Mail*. "Denis would have had to scale five six-foot-high fences to get there and back.

"I have never tried to stop his behavior. I would much rather he bring objects into the house than dead animals," Newman said.

Newman, 48, said it's not uncommon for neighbors to come over to reclaim their missing possessions. "A few people have knocked on the door to ask if Denis has stolen their things, but thankfully, no one has been angry yet," she told the BBC. Because of his antics, the neighbors altered his name from just Denis to Denis the Menace.

The cat criminal has gained a huge fan base and become a hit on the web. In addition to his own Facebook page and Twitter account, he also has a YouTube channel that features videos of the feline felon returning home with his latest stolen items. He even has his own line of T-shirts, including one that reads "Denis stole my pants." Profits from the sale of the T-shirts and from advertising on his YouTube channel go to Homeless Cat Rescue Bedfordshire.

Perhaps inspired by Denis the Menace, another English family cat went on a year-long crime spree to also earn a new nickname — Naughty Norris.

In 2012, the lovable one-year-old tabby suddenly turned into a clever cat burglar. Going out through a cat door, he began sneaking into yards, garages, and even homes to swipe everything from clothes to food in the Bedminster area of Bristol, England.

"He was perfectly well behaved up until the age of one, but then he started to turn to a life of petty crime," his owner, Richard Windsor, 26, a graphic designer, told the *Bristol Post* in 2013. "He started bringing things in from the recycling bins. At first it was just the odd thing," such as a dustcloth, dishrag, mop head, and bath mat.

"We have even had a pair of washing-up gloves, each brought in on a separate night."

But then, Windsor said, "he really started to up his game." As his thieving ways grew stronger, Naughty Norris began taking more expensive items, bringing home sports bras, tights, sweaters, T-shirts, and boxer shorts. Many of the things he snatched came from clotheslines.

"He goes out in the evening and then returns quite late, sometimes in the early hours," Windsor told the newspaper. "He brings his stolen items in and then meows and meows to announce he is back, so we will go and see what he has brought in. Sometimes he will go out multiple times during one night."

Whenever the cat brought home a swiped item that was too big for the cat flap, he would leave it on the mat in the backyard for Windsor and his wife, Sophie, to find in the morning.

Apparently, burglarizing the neighborhood worked up quite an appetite for the cat because Naughty Norris also brought home half a pizza, an unopened tube of gravy paste, and a German sausage.

"At first we thought it was funny," Windsor said. "But as his stash grew and the items were getting bigger, we thought we needed to return them. It is not as if they are high-value items, but they all belong to someone."

Deciding to reunite the cat's booty with the victims, the couple wrote a note to their neighbors that said in part: "This is a slightly embarrassing note to have to write, but during his travels throughout the neighborhood, our cat, Norris, has brought back an assortment of items. Unlike most cats, Norris isn't too interested in the local wildlife, but has taken to straight-up theft. . . . We now have a growing pile of stolen goods which need returning to you good people of Bedminster. . . . If you've 'misplaced' anything of any monetary value and would like it returned, then please give us a nudge. We'll have a dig through his growing hoard and drop them back to you. Apologies if you've been affected."

The couple was able to return a number of items — including a towel set, oven gloves, bath mat, baby clothes, and running gear — to their owners. "Fortunately, all our neighbors have been very good-natured about it and think it is funny," Windsor told the *Bristol Post*. "At least now they know where to come if something disappears mysteriously."

It's as if cats like Norris and Denis don't die; they just "steal away."

NOT PLAYING THE FAIR WAY

A sly raccoon victimized golfers by creeping up to their golf carts and stealing their purses and items from their golf bags while the players were focused on their next shot.

During the spring of 2011, officials and golfers at the Sandridge Golf Club in Vero Beach, Florida, were mystified how a thief could steal purses, wallets, and golf balls from golfers out on the fairway without being seen.

Golfer Eunice Messick had just started her round on the club's Dunes Course when she walked back to her cart and noticed her purse had vanished. She filed a police report, canceled her credit cards, got new keys made, and changed the locks on her house. Meanwhile, other golfers noticed that the pockets on their golf bags had been unzipped and items were missing, usually around the first green.

The thief was finally identified about a week later when a woman golfer on the first hole just happened to look behind her. "She saw the raccoon grab her purse, take it from the golf cart, and carry it into the bushes," Bob Komarinetz, Sandridge's director of golf at the time, told WPTV-TV.

After groundskeepers were alerted, they searched the area where the raccoon was last seen waddling into the bushes. They soon found the masked bandit's hideaway. Stashed in a little clearing surrounded by brush were Messick's purse and the other woman's purse. Groundskeepers also recovered several stolen golf balls and wrappers from snacks taken from golf bags.

The thief, however, was nowhere to be found.

A few days later, the raccoon attempted another theft. Golfer Bob Albrightson was getting ready to putt on the first hole when he looked behind him and saw the raccoon sitting on his golf cart. Albrightson chased him off and then noticed his golf bag had been unzipped. "I looked on the ground and there was my wallet," he told WPTV. "And he had taken a ball out of my bag as well."

A woman golfer who had brought some cupcakes to share with her playing partners was also victimized by the sneaky bandit. He grabbed the box of goodies and was trying to make his getaway when the golfer yelled and ran after him. The thief dropped the box and disappeared into the bushes.

Fed up with the thefts, golf course officials tried to capture the criminal, but he was too wily for them. In their first attempt, they set up a humane trap and baited it with a can of tuna. But the cunning critter tipped over the cage and then ate all the tuna. Next, they staked down the cage so it couldn't be tipped over and baited it again. But the rascally raccoon simply dug under the trap to get at the food.

"We had traps out there a number of times, and we had professional trappers come out, too," Bela Nagy, then manager of golf operations at Sandridge, told TCPalm.com. "We couldn't trap the guy. He's too smart."

Later that summer, officials called off efforts to trap the thief, who was occasionally seen hanging out by the golf club's south practice area. Judging from the lack of reports of thefts on the course, it seemed the crooked raccoon had mended his ways. Meanwhile, club officials were dealing with a weightier problem — wild pigs had been milling around in the out-of-bounds area and hogging all the attention.

ON THE BALL

Players at a Swiss golf course were losing balls on certain holes, but it wasn't because of their bad shots. It was because a bad fox had been swiping them.

In a rough estimate, the bushy-tailed red fox stole about one hundred golf balls on the fairway at the Verbier

Golf Club's Par 3 Moulins course, sparking both annoyance and chuckles from his victims.

Foxy, as the thief has been named, first showed up in fall 2013. He hid in the bushes on certain holes every day between 4 P.M. and 6 P.M. After a golfer hit his drive down the fairway, Foxy would scamper onto the course, pick up the ball, and run off with it into the woods. He committed his crimes alone.

For hard-core golfers, Foxy's crime wave was no laughing matter. Not only did he disrupt their games but he was also taking their favorite and, in some cases, expensive golf balls.

"He's running around in between holes one and six, waiting for the players to hit the ball and then directly he is running after the ball and running away with it in his mouth," the club's director, Thomas Grech, told CNN at the time. "We do not know where the balls are. He has a few [hiding places] around the golf course. People have looked for them, but there's no chance [in finding them].

"Of course the fox is disturbing the game," he added. "But most people are not angry at all. He is just trying to play with the golfers."

Although Foxy teed off some golfers, he amused many others, who were able to "putt" it all behind them.

In fact, golfers deliberately asked for afternoon tee times, hoping Foxy would steal their golf balls so they would have a funny story to tell their friends.

"It's more a game for the fox," Grech said. "He is tricky, but we like the little fox. People are interested in him, and many people come in the afternoon to see the animal. My colleague Muriel Guex, who looks after the restaurant, tells me she has more people in between four and six o'clock for when the fox comes."

Judging from his appearance and behavior, Foxy seemed healthy and not intimidated by humans, even golfers who chased after him and yelled at him.

"The story has gone around the world," said Grech. "It's very, very funny." Well, that's a "fore"-gone conclusion.

GRIN AND BEAR IT

A bear was breaking into cars in a small Canadian town, but not by smashing windows. No, this crafty bruin knew how to use the door handles to gain entry and steal whatever goodies he could find inside.

Rebecca Moore, of Maple Ridge, British Columbia, told the Canadian Broadcasting Corporation (CBC) that she and her husband were awakened about 5:30 A.M. one morning in 2013 by a strange noise. When they looked out their window, they were shocked to see a bear on his hind legs trying to open the door to her minivan.

"By the time we got out of bed, the bear was actually inside my car," she told the CBC. "The passenger door was open, and at first we thought he had left." But the car began rocking back and forth from the bear's weight, so they knew he was still inside. Then he got out the passenger door and opened the sliding side door of the minivan and climbed back in.

Not finding anything worth stealing in the vehicle, the bear exited and ambled over to Moore's husband's four-door pickup truck.

"We saw him just open the door of the truck," she told the CBC. "He was obviously used to accessing vehicles. We just thought it was hilarious."

Before running out of the house to scare him off, Moore grabbed her camera and began shooting video of the bear. "You just couldn't believe what you were seeing," she said. "It was just too amazing not to take a video."

Moore posted video of the burglarizing bear on YouTube. The video shows the thief climbing out of the truck on the passenger's side, opening up the door to the back seat as easily as a human would, and climbing in, no doubt looking for food. But there was nothing for him to steal.

"He is obviously quite a pro and has done this many times," Moore told the CBC. "This wasn't the first time. He knew what he was doing."

After shooting video of the lumbering criminal, Moore and her husband chased him away. "This was just so amazing to see how easy he could access the vehicles," she said. "I'd never seen anything quite so brazen."

A wildlife official said the bear, estimated to be about three years old, was suspected of being a repeat offender. Conservation officer Denny Chretien told the CBC that he had received four reports of a bear breaking into a vehicle, including an expensive Porsche. Fortunately, none of the owners had left the key in the ignition.

NOTHING TO CROW ABOUT

Crows turned into grinches when they began stealing ornaments from two outdoor community Christmas trees.

Following a tradition in the town of Lakeside, Oregon, volunteers decorated donated Christmas trees with themes that reflected various community organizations in 2009. The trees, which were set up outside the city hall, featured mostly handmade ornaments, trinkets, and little toys.

Resident Sheli Roe helped fire chief Ted Ross make fire-fighting-themed ornaments for the Lakeside Rural Protection District tree, while other volunteers decked out the senior center tree by hanging painted recycled prescription pill bottles.

Shortly after the trees were decorated, ornaments began disappearing off the two trees. First, toy vehicles, including a tiny motorcycle, vanished from the fire-district tree. Then foam fire badges and miniature red, wooden fire hydrants were missing. Ornaments from the senior tree disappeared, too.

That ruffled the feathers of the townspeople. "It's sad, is what you're thinking," Roe told *The World*, the local newspaper in Coos Bay. "It's Christmas, and someone would steal Christmas ornaments?"

People assumed it was a thief who didn't like the holidays. But then Ross found one of the pill-bottle ornaments lying on the street near city hall. Later, he came across the missing toy motorcycle ornament. He looked around and noticed several crows nearby.

"All I could see was something bright red in the crows' feet as they were flying off," Ross told the newspaper. "That's when we realized that our perpetrators were small critters."

Ross said he figured the birds were hungry, and they thought the bright, sparkling ornaments might be something to eat. "A crow is an animal of opportunity," he said. "If it sees something it thinks it can eat, it will check it out."

Roe said she recalled a crow stealing a bright orange egg during the previous year's community Easter egg hunt, but she didn't link the two cases. "It never occurred to us that the crows would take little metal cars," she told the newspaper.

After learning of the identity of the thieves, Roe made new ornaments with craft items she found at home and replenished the tree, even though it was quite a "birden." This time, though, she tied them on as tightly as she could. She told the newspaper, "They're going to have to take the whole tree to get them."

UNDERGROUND MOVEMENT

Unpatriotic woodchucks were stealing American flags from the gravesites of Civil War veterans — committing their brazen crimes in the days leading up to America's most patriotic holiday.

Shortly before Independence Day 2012, police in

Hudson, New York, were investigating the theft of 75 miniature flags that volunteers had placed at the Civil War-era tombstones in the Grand Army of the Republic section of the Hudson City Cemetery. Officials in the town and the cemetery were convinced that thoughtless vandals were swiping the little flags.

The police department of the small town took the crime seriously and assigned four patrolmen to the case. The cops conducted stakeouts and used bike patrols in an effort to catch the thieves in the act. When police failed to turn up any leads, they set up motion-detector cameras in the cemetery, and the effort paid off. The cameras revealed that the recurring crime was an inside job perpetrated by underground residents of the cemetery — woodchucks.

"I think for the most part we've confirmed that's the case," Mayor Bill Hallenbeck told the *Register-Star*. Still photos from a motion-activated camera showed a woodchuck at a flag. "Shortly after this, another [photo] showed the flag was gone," the mayor said. Teeth marks were seen on the tiny flagpole.

He said police then used a special camera attached to a pole to check woodchuck holes in the cemetery. "They confirmed there are flags down there." The black-and-white images identified pieces of flags in several holes. It was now obvious that the animals had nibbled on the flags and dragged them into their dens.

There had been a whole underground network of flag stealers. During the investigation, police learned that other municipalities were having similar problems with woodchucks or groundhogs stealing miniature flags. The flags most likely to be taken were ones coated with a substance that attracted the varmints, Hallenbeck said.

Volunteers finally put an end to the woodchucks' crime wave by installing new three-foot-high flag posts at the Civil War graves, which put the flags out of reach of the furry filchers.

Now there's no way to know how many flags would a woodchuck chuck if a woodchuck could chuck flags.

RASCALS

DRIVING WITHOUT A LICENSE

Left alone in his owner's car, Toby the Chihuahua just couldn't resist going for a joyride. It didn't end well. He bumped into another car.

Jason Martinez, of Spokane, Washington, had brought his tan-colored dog with him as he ran some errands one winter day in 2014. At one stop, Martinez parked in front of a store and went inside, leaving Toby in the car.

For such a little pooch, Toby soon got into big trouble.

Figuring it would be a doggone shame not to take advantage of this moment, Toby got behind the steering wheel, knocked the gear selector into neutral, and then

34

"drove off" as the vehicle rolled down the street. His escapade would have lasted longer had Toby not driven into another auto.

Driver Tabitha Ormaechea was behind the wheel of her car, which was stopped at a red light at a busy intersection in Spokane, when Toby's vehicle struck the woman's rear tire and wheel well.

"Out of nowhere I had looked at all the lights, no cars, so I reached down to get some ChapStick, and that's when I got hit," Ormaechea told KREM-TV. "When I looked up, there was no one in the other car, just a little dog up on the steering wheel peeking over and looking at me. I was shocked. I didn't know if I was crazy, or if this little dog had taken a joyride."

Of course, that's exactly what had happened.

Meanwhile, Martinez was still in the store, unaware of his dog's outing until a witness spoke up. "Someone ran into the store and asked if anyone had a brown car, and I said, 'Yeah, me. Why?'" Martinez told KREM. "I didn't know what to think."

Martinez said he had been in the store for just a few minutes before Toby got into car trouble. "He must have knocked it out of gear, and the car rolled out," he said.

Fortunately, no one was hurt and the damage was minimal. Luckily for Toby, Martinez was not hot under the collar over this tail of woe, although he was seen "mutt"-ering to himself.

BAD CALL

A cat named Bruce Lee made an emergency call to police, who then rushed to the residence and busted the door to gain entry — only to discover there was no real crisis other than what the feline had caused.

James Cocksedge, 33, of the Camden borough of London, England, and his fiancée, Monica de la Cruz, had gone to work one day in 2013, leaving their Singapura kittens Bruce Lee and Audrey home alone. A few hours later, a 999 call (the same as a 911 call in the United States) was made from Cocksedge's apartment.

The dispatcher couldn't get anyone to respond, so police were sent to investigate. When they knocked on the door, they heard what sounded like shrieking. Fearing that someone was being attacked, they battered open the door and rushed inside, where they found Bruce Lee and Audrey wrestling with each other. Seeing the cops, Bruce Lee took off and hid under a pile of clothes in the closet.

When Cocksedge came home for lunch, he was stunned to find his door was damaged and police were inside his apartment. "They said, 'Don't worry, we've had to force entry, but the cat is all right,'" Cocksedge told the *Camden New Journal*.

"The phone was on the floor. Audrey was quite relaxed, but Bruce Lee had disappeared," he added. It didn't take long for Cocksedge to solve the case. "I found Bruce looking guilty at the back of the wardrobe, and I put two and two together."

Ever since Cocksedge had a landline installed in the apartment, Bruce Lee would rush to answer the phone whenever it rang. He also became fascinated by the buttons, which he loved to press. "Basically, he always jumps when the phone rings and then starts knocking about the receiver," Cocksedge explained to the newspaper.

"I imagine someone must have rung, and Bruce probably went nuts. He dialed nine three times, heard a voice, suddenly freaked out, and left the phone. Then the police started banging down the door and he hid."

The yowling the police heard when they broke into the apartment came from the two cats having a spat. Bruce Lee and Audrey are pedigree Singapuras, a breed known for being active and playful.

Cocksedge said he didn't blame the police for damaging the door, which cost several hundred dollars to repair. "They were just doing their job."

He didn't get mad at Bruce Lee, either. "I couldn't," he said. "He already looked so ashamed of himself. He got himself into this situation and then didn't know what to do, so he just hid. If anything, I felt a lot of sympathy for him. He was quite upset by the whole ordeal. It happened the day before his first birthday, so it wasn't great timing for Brucie."

On the day of the ordeal, he told the newspaper, "Bruce Lee is still in shock. We've been cuddling him, rubbing his belly, prodding him, throwing his favorite balls so he can fetch them. He likes that. But we've also started to unplug the phone when we're out. He's got a cheeky side to him, and he might do it again, although he'd be silly to try."

If there is a next time, Bruce Lee might get charged with a "feliney."

STINKER OF A GAME

A skunk that tried to join a sideline huddle during a tense high school football game played a key role in the team's heartbreaking defeat.

There has never been any love lost between the Baldwyn Bearcats and Booneville Blue Devils, two rival schools in Prentiss County, Mississippi. In 2012, the Bearcats were hoping to put an end to the Blue Devils' three-game winning streak against them. And it looked as if Baldwyn just might do it, after going into half time with a 27–7 lead.

But Booneville fought back in the second half and trailed 27–21 midway through the fourth quarter. With momentum on the Blue Devils' side, the Bearcats called a time-out to regroup. They desperately wanted to hold on and avoid another loss to their archenemy.

Unfortunately for them, that's when a little stinker made a big stink.

During the time-out, a skunk ran onto the field. It reached the 20-yard line before it stopped, as if wondering which sideline to go to. Booneville coach Mike Mattox, who had seen the skunk roaming near the end zone earlier, decided he wasn't going to allow the critter on his sideline. Admitting to being superstitious and no fan of skunks, he charged toward the critter to keep it away from his players. "I thought, 'If it sprays me or whatever, I'm kicking it to the other side if I have to,'" he told the local newspaper, the *North Eastern Mississippi Daily Journal*.

The skunk didn't want anything to do with Mattox,

so it turned tail and scampered toward the Baldwyn sideline, where the Bearcats were huddling around their coach. Suddenly, half the team ran to the right and the other half to the left, forming a wide, clear path for the skunk. "It was like the parting of the Red Sea over there," Mattox recalled.

"We were already in a time-out, and the skunk just started running toward us," Baldwyn senior Devonta Gates told the *Daily Journal*. "The only thing I knew was run."

Cheerleaders on the sideline screamed and bolted. Not finding any love from the players or cheerleaders, the skunk ran under the bleachers, causing mayhem in the stands as panicked fans cleared out in fear of getting sprayed. Fortunately for them, the spurned skunk didn't resort to his smelly weapon.

When order was restored, the shaken Bearcats sensed that the skunk was a bad omen. It was. The Blue Devils' Andrew Lambert intercepted a pass on the Booneville 16-yard line and returned it 84 yards for the winning touchdown. Baldwyn lost, 28–27.

"I've been accused of bringing the skunk and turning it loose," Mattox told the newspaper. "I've heard from everywhere. I even had a radio station in San Diego call."

In one of his least favorite things to do, Baldwyn coach Michael Gray watched film of his team's fourth straight loss to Booneville. "The skunk was just roaming back and forth in the end zone," he told the *Daily Journal*. "It got up to the twenty-yard line one time. I remember it coming right between a handful of us . . . then we commenced to getting beat."

Even though it didn't make a lot of "scents," video of the critter's dramatic play on the field went viral, including on YouTube, ESPN, and *Good Morning America*. The game has since been dubbed the Skunk Bowl.

ROO-ING THE DAY

Wanting to play on the golf course, kangaroos by leaps and bounds swarmed onto the fairway, temporarily halting a prestigious international tournament.

In what will go down as one of the strangest delays in golf history, the kangaroos bounded onto the course at the Royal Canberra Golf Club, interrupting the first round of the 2013 LPGA Handa Australian Open. They couldn't care less that they were stopping play of the best women golfers in the world. All the roos wanted to do was just have a little fun.

The animals had been seen in the area throughout the previous week, although they weren't so bold as to storm the course. But all that changed when golfer Karrie Webb was getting ready to strike her ball from the fairway on the ninth hole. Suddenly, out of nowhere, more than 30 kangaroos emerged from the rough, hopped right in front of her, and then jumped, mingled, and frolicked on the course. There was nothing that Webb or the other golfers could do but shake their heads and laugh. Being from Australia, Webb was used to seeing kangaroos, but not this many . . . especially on a golf course . . . during a major tournament.

Eventually, after several minutes, the marsupials went on their way, and play resumed — at least for the humans.

The hoppers — identified as eastern grey kangaroos — usually frequent grasslands, but were drawn to the lush conditions on the course because the region was experiencing exceptionally hot, dry conditions.

The golfers took the surprise invasion in stride. Canadian golfer Rebecca Lee-Bentham tweeted, "First time seeing kangaroos on the golf course!" Taiwanese golfer Yani Tseng tweeted, "Wow, so many kangaroos!!! I'm playing golf in the zoo."

FOWL PLAY

A Kansas City Royals' loss to the Cleveland Indians was for the birds — literally. The defeat was caused, in part, by a stubborn seagull.

At a major league game in Cleveland in 2012, the two teams were tied 3–3 going into the bottom of the tenth inning. The Indians had runners Mark DeRosa on second base and Victor Martinez on first.

Aside from the players, the field also was occupied by a flock of seagulls who were lounging in center field. The gulls, fattening themselves on bugs at the ballpark, had been swarming throughout the game and had ignored players' earlier attempts to leave.

So, when Cleveland batter Shin-Soo Choo came up to bat, the feathered fans were still relaxing in center field for a bird's-eye view of the game. Choo singled sharply up the middle, straight toward the seagulls. The ball bounded into the outfield where Royals center fielder Coco Crisp was getting into position to scoop it up and hurl it home, hoping to throw DeRosa out at the plate.

But while other birds got out of Crisp's way, one gull refused to move. It didn't even duck. The ball struck the bird and was deflected away from the outfielder at a "hawkward" angle. As the ball rolled to the outfield wall, DeRosa easily scored the winning run. After getting hit by the ball, the stunned seagull wobbled around for a while before finally regaining its senses and taking flight. It left behind a feather on the outfield grass as the victorious Indians congratulated one another on the bird-brained win.

Crisp raised his arms in frustration, claiming the seagull had interfered with the play. But umpire Mike Reilly, citing the rule book, confirmed that any ball striking a bird in fair territory is considered in play and not "fowl." The game was over . . . and the Royals lost, thanks to the seagull "robin" them of a chance at victory.

Like most of the Royals, Crisp thought the result of the play was for the birds. "The ball was hit so sharply that I had a chance to throw the runner out," he claimed after the game.

Reilly, who was umpiring first base, told reporters he thought Crisp had a shot at gunning down the runner. "Believe me, we [the umpires] talked about it when we came in," Reilly said. "There probably would have been a play at the plate had not there been interference by the bird. There's nothing we can do about those things."

Choo was delighted that the seagull played a major role in the win. "The bird helped," he said. "I'll take it."

Apparently, having fun at the Royals' expense, the seagull was acting more like a mockingbird.

MEDIA HOG

Parker the pig hammed it up during a minor league baseball game in 2013, sending the crowd squealing in hysterics by running around the field and halting play.

Parker is a "rally pig" for the Richmond (Virginia) Flying Squirrels. During the late innings of home games when the team is trailing, he makes an appearance. He is put in a special two-wheeled farm cart pulled by Farmer Larry, a guy wearing overalls and a straw hat. The pig is wheeled around the field from the first base side to the third base side.

On this particular evening, with the Flying Squirrels trailing 7–4, Parker was brought out in his cart. But then a member of the opposing team, the Bowie (Maryland) Baysox, "accidentally" ran into the cart, allowing Parker to get out.

Seizing the limelight, the pig scampered onto the diamond, delaying the start of the bottom of the seventh inning. Larry and a couple of members from the grounds crew went after him, but he proved more elusive than they thought. Even the team's mascot, Nutzy — someone clad in a black, red, and gray squirrel costume — went after the pig. So did a couple of players.

But no one was a match for Parker the porker, who started toward shortslop . . . er . . . shortstop before reversing direction. He eluded everyone, surprising them with his speed and ability to fake out his pursuers. Finally, though, he realized it behooved him to quit his antics, so he trotted off the field on his own.

Parker's moment of glory brought him a brief burst of national attention. Video of his escape even made it on ESPN's *SportsCenter* — on the "Not the Top Ten" plays of the week.

TERRI-BULL

Incensed that he had been taken to a cattle market, a bull broke free, galloped through a small town in Ireland, and charged into — of all places — a supermarket, causing customers and workers to flee in all directions.

It all began on market day in 2009 in Ballinrobe, County Mayo. As the bull was being led into the cattle ring to be sold, he proved he was like no udder . . . um . . . other. He broke free from his owner, jumped out of the ring, and hoofed it up the main street while the owner and other people ran after him.

The bull trotted for a half mile past a Tesco supermarket, turned left, then right, and came straight through the automatic double doors of Cummins' SuperValu. As shocked patrons and employees got out of his way, the beast turned the store into a "flee" market. He skidded and slid down one aisle and then another to the rear of the store where some of the workers — including a butcher, naturally — bravely tried to block him with some shopping carts. The bull wasn't amused but turned around anyway.

Meanwhile, security cameras showed the bull's owner racing into the store down the main aisle. But when he saw the animal rushing toward him, the man spun on his heels and dashed out of there as fast as he could, with the bull in hot pursuit. Incredibly, the bull did little damage other than knock over a few fruit and vegetable displays.

"He went straight through the shop, out into the store, had a good look about, turned around, and went straight out again," store owner John Cummins told *The Guardian*. "I could not believe my eyes.

"There were a lot of people in the shop at the time, staff and customers. It was a happy ending to a story that could have gone very wrong. Thank goodness no one was injured." Employee Helen McDonnell told the newspaper, "I could smell the bull, and when he was charging out again I never moved so fast in my life."

The bull was eventually captured by the owner, a local farmer, who brought the animal back to the cattle market.

His escapade in the store was captured on video by security cameras and put on YouTube, where it went viral. "It's amazing the comments we have been getting," because of the video, Cummins said. "One customer said he had had a call from a relative in Sydney [Australia] and another from a brother in Hong Kong."

People were joking that Cummins had the freshest beef in town.

BAD CATTITUDE

Some cats love to harass TV crews, apparently in a bid to get seen on television.

For example, in 2013 CBC cameraman Sam Martin was covering a story with reporter Briar Stewart about school buses. The pair was standing on a snowy street in Bonnyville, Alberta, where Martin had set up his camera to shoot Stewart's report. Suddenly, they were surprised by an unexpected visitor from the neighborhood.

Wanting to get the attention of the cameraman, a gray-and-white tabby with a red collar leaped onto Martin's back while he was shooting Stewart's promo for the story. The cameraman remained cool and kept shooting, so the cat took more drastic measures to get his attention and moved from Martin's shoulders to the top of his head. When that didn't work, the media-friendly feline perched on the tripod-mounted camera as if to say, "You can't ignore me now."

Off-camera, Martin chuckled and said, "Is this for real?"

Stewart lost her composure and burst out laughing. "I have never seen that in my life!" she said. "Somebody needs to videotape this." CBC field producer Terry Reith managed to snap multiple shots of the wanting-to-get-on-TV cat.

After Martin gently took the feline off the camera, the crew finished the report. Disappointed that it didn't get on live TV, the cat jumped onto the hood of the news team's car, walked up to the driver's side windshield, and engaged in a stare down with Martin, who was behind the wheel.

In the end, the cat got more media attention than it could ever have imagined. Photos of it went viral.

Stewart said the entire incident would have been funnier if the cat had done to her what it did to Martin during her live report.

In fact, a cat did exactly that to a reporter in Grand Rapids, Michigan, a year earlier.

Nicole DiDonato, of WXMI-TV, was getting ready to do a live promo (also known as a tease) outside for her upcoming story about a microbrewery when she noticed a curious gray cat walking nearby. DiDonato smiled at it and then turned to face the camera.

As she checked to see if her microphone was working, the crew back in the studio could hear her voice fine — as well as loud meowing in the background. Then DiDonato began her live tease. As the TV audience watched in amusement, a cat's paw emerged over the reporter's left shoulder. DiDonato's eyes grew wide, but with impressive professionalism, she kept talking without missing a beat — even though the attention-seeking cat climbed right onto her shoulder and perched there for the rest of the promo.

As soon as she finished the live tease, DiDonato doubled over and began to laugh, and so did the anchorwomen back in the studio. The audience at home watched, too, as the cat remained perched on her shoulder for its brief moment of fame. The video went viral.

Later, DiDonato tweeted, "Learned my lesson: Never making eye contact with a cat before a live tease ever again."

HO, HO, NO!

One of Santa's reindeer went dashing through the snow without the big man and disappeared for a day.

In 2013 Santa had arrived in Dillon, Colorado, with one of his reindeer for the town's annual lighting celebration, an evening of festivities that included crafts, holiday music, and an appearance by the jolly man in red and one of his reindeer. Portraying Santa was Bill Lee, owner of the Laughing Valley Ranch in Idaho Springs. As he had in the past, he brought one of his domesticated reindeer with him so that children could pet the animal and take pictures with it outside the La Riva Mall in downtown Dillon.

But on this night, something spooked the reindeer. So while Santa Claus was inside the mall listening to children's Christmas wishes, the reindeer jerked its lead rope away from its handler, jumped over the enclosure, and bolted through town.

That led to one of the strangest holiday sights ever seen in Dillon. There was Santa Claus — along with the handler, the police, and an animal control officer — chasing after his runaway reindeer. Even without Rudolph guiding it, the reindeer galloped through the streets of Dillon and disappeared into the night. The pursuers noticed that its tracks stopped at the shoreline of Lake Dillon, which meant that it had swum into the lake. Without any further sign of the animal on land or water, the searchers gave up for the night.

However, early the next morning, Dillon police received a call from a man who said he was walking his dogs along the shoreline when he spotted a reindeer with a halter and lead rope walking on a nearby trail.

When Dillon police officer Bryan Wagner arrived at work, he was given an unusual assignment — find the missing reindeer and bring it back safely. "I came up here from Florida," Wagner later told the *Summit Daily News*. "We used to wrestle with alligators all the time. But reindeer is new."

So Wagner, Lee (without his Santa suit), and several other volunteers mounted another search for the reindeer. A few hours later, they found it and tried to corner it, but the animal eluded them and disappeared again. Figuring that it was extremely frightened and didn't know what to do, Lee came up with a new strategy. When the runaway was spotted again, Lee arrived on the scene with another reindeer from his ranch, hoping that a familiar face would help lure the scared animal.

The plan worked to perfection. The lost reindeer began to follow its four-legged pal down the road until the searchers grabbed its lead rope and guided it into a trailer. Santa got an early Christmas gift — the safe return of his wayward animal, one that no longer had "free rein."

EXTREME SCREAM

Charcoal the goat was all fired up and angry that he had been separated from his buddies, so he protested the only way he knew how. He began bleating loudly. The problem was that he sounded exactly like a person screaming for help.

Yes, you can guess what happened next. Fearing that someone was in danger, a neighbor called the police, who rushed to the scene. Imagine the cops' surprise when they discovered the "screaming" was coming from a goat — an irate one.

When Maria Reneau, of Baxter, Tennessee, arrived home from work one evening in 2013, she stepped out of her car and was startled to hear a frantic cry. From somewhere in the wooded rural neighborhood, Reneau thought she heard a person yelling, "Heeeelp! Heeeelp!"

Being a concerned citizen, Reneau picked up the phone and called 911. "She said it sounded like someone was dying or saying 'help,'" Jacky Farley, chief deputy of the Putnam County Sheriff's Department, told WTVF-TV.

Deputies rushed to the area where they, too, heard the cries of distress that sounded exactly like those of someone in peril. They couldn't help but laugh after they soon discovered that the yells were coming from Charcoal the goat. He was tied up to a post, still bleating at the top of his lungs.

Reneau's neighbor, Carlos Mendez, told deputies that his one-year-old goat was upset with him and wanted him to know it. "He's used to being with the other goats, and we separated him," Mendez told WSMV-TV. "I guess he didn't want to be alone so he wanted to get back with the other goats."

Meanwhile, the goat was the butt of jokes around the neighborhood.

ESCAPE ARTIST

A pet dog named Rope earned the new nickname "Houdini" after he did what no other animal at a high-security Colorado shelter had ever done before — escape. And that was no easy feat.

Rope, a clever and mischievous five-year-old Australian shepherd, had a habit of opening unlocked doors at his home whenever his human family wasn't looking. He would amble off and then return later in the day. But one time in 2013 he didn't come back. Despite searching for days, the owners couldn't find him. However, someone did capture the wayward dog. Because Rope didn't have a collar, tags, or an identification chip, he was taken to the Humane Society of the Pikes Peak Region (HSPPR) in Colorado Springs, Colorado.

Rope was tired of waiting to be reunited with his family and escaped in the middle of the night. The next day, staffers at the shelter were mystified by his disappearance, so they checked the overnight video from their surveillance cameras. What they saw astonished them.

Through determination, a little luck, and lots of smarts, the dog had managed to break out of his kennel.

Then the cameras caught him opening not one but two doors to gain his freedom around 1 A.M.

"He had to actually push down the handle, push the door open, and walk out in both cases," Gretchen Pressley, the humane society's communications specialist, told KKTV-TV. "He let himself out of the kennel room about midnight and let himself out of the building. No animal has ever gotten through the door into the rest of the shelter before. This was new for us."

Rope walked for about a mile until he was found early the next morning by Ashley Heister. Seeing that he had a tag from the humane society, she brought him back to the shelter. She told staffers that if no one claimed him, she wanted to adopt him, because she and the rest of her family had already fallen in love with him. They even gave him a name — Houdini — in honor of the famous escape artist.

Following its policy, the shelter required a waiting period before an unidentified animal in its care could be put up for adoption. During this time, the dog's remarkable breakout made the news on local television. On the last day before Heister could adopt the dog, Rope's owners appeared at the shelter and were reunited with their wandering pet. They said they had been looking for Rope and had almost given up hope of finding him until they saw the story of his escape on TV.

The humane society micro chipped the dog free of charge because of his strong tendency to escape. To make sure that Rope won't go on another unauthorized trek, his owners said they would keep a close eye on the clever pooch — and double-check that all their doors were kept locked.

INTRUDERS

A SWEET DEAL

A young black bear with a sweet tooth found the perfect place to burglarize — a candy factory. He then proceeded to gorge himself on chocolate treats.

Late one night in 2012, the bear strolled by the closed-for-the-day Rocky Mountain Chocolate Factory in Estes Park, Colorado. Getting a whiff of the candy inside, he tried opening the locked front door. Like Yogi Bear, this bruin was smarter than your average bear. He slipped his claws under the door and was able to pop it open because it was secured by only a faulty lock. Once inside the shop, he ate goodies to his heart's content and then left without breaking a thing.

When shop owner Jo Adams came to work the next morning, she noticed a candy tin and a cellophane wrapper on the floor, and dirt on top of the checkout counter. She later told the *Estes Parks News*, "I thought, 'Oh darn, one of those pesky squirrels has gotten in the store and upset a few things.'"

Jo summoned her son, Eric, to help her find the squirrel and clean up before she opened the store. When their search failed to find any critter, Eric watched video from the store's four surveillance cameras. That's when he discovered the real culprit was a young bear.

The video showed the bear taking a mouthful of candy from the display rack at the counter, walking out the door, and then eating it on the sidewalk. As soon as he finished, he went back inside for another helping of treats, which he took outside again before munching on them. He repeated this same routine, going in and out of the shop, seven times during his twenty-minute-long burglary.

The bear was careful not to damage anything. At one point, he hopped over the counter, ambled behind a sealed candy case, jumped up onto the back counter, and strolled along it, stepping over items without disturbing a single thing. He also placed his paws gently on the glass candy-display case, leaving only his paw prints.

When he had his fill, he walked out of the store — no doubt with a sugar high.

"That little bugger ate a lot of candy!" Adams told the newspaper. The bear's favorite things were the chocolate-covered Rice Krispies Treats, peanut butter cups, a special Rocky Mountain Chocolate Factory candy called Balls of Joy, English toffee, and some cookies dipped in caramel and milk chocolate called . . . what else? . . . Cookie Bears.

After discovering that the bear had broken into her shop, Adams, family members, and employees cleaned and disinfected the counters and displays and threw out any candy that the bear might have been in contact with. The lock was replaced, too.

The next night, the bear returned, but this time he couldn't break into the shop because of the new lock, so he quit trying and left behind his calling card — some muddy paw prints on the front door.

In an ironic twist, the burglary was good for business. As word of the bear break-in spread, customers began ordering the same treats that the bear had enjoyed. "At least five times a day people come in to order the exact same things the bear ate," Adams told the newspaper at the time. "I love it. We've been making extras of these particular treats just to keep up with the demand."

MAKING HIMSELF AT HOME

A bear nicknamed Blue was looking for a place to hibernate in the Montana woods. Unlike his fellow bruins, he decided against a cold den or dark cave. No, he had bigger plans than that.

The 200-pound bear chose to spend the winter of 2012 in the crawl space under a family's vacation cabin. Not only that, but he stole their sheets, blankets, comforters, and pillows, and piled them in his little makeshift den to stay cozy and warm.

Judy Wing, of Missoula, Montana, who owns the cabin on Georgetown Lake, had no idea that Blue had taken up residence underneath her home. When members of her family went to stay there on New Year's Day, they found the place had been ransacked. At first, they assumed that a burglar had broken into the cabin, even though the doors and windows were locked and weren't damaged in any way.

When they began cleaning up the mess, they noticed something wasn't right: Nothing of value had been taken — not the television, satellite dish, kitchenware, or artwork. The only things missing were the bedding and pillows. "We thought that was really weird," recalled family member Byron Schmaus.

He told the *Billings Gazette* that the next morning they noticed pillows had been stuffed down into the crawl space. The family thought that one or more raccoons had pilfered the pillows. Schmaus told the newspaper that his father-in-law took a flashlight and opened an unlatched hatch in the floor that led to the crawl space. When he stuck his head down there, he saw a pair of large eyes staring back at him from four feet away — and they weren't those of a raccoon. "You couldn't get him [his father-in-law] out of that hold fast enough," Schmaus told the *Gazette*.

The family reckoned that after the bear had crawled under the cabin, he figured out how to open the hatch to gain access to the place and then swiped the bedding.

Schmaus promptly nailed the hatch shut and called the Montana Department of Fish, Wildlife & Parks, which sent out a game warden to assess the situation. The warden told Wing that he didn't have enough space to shoot a tranquilizer dart at the bear without ripping up some of the floorboards. She was not willing to damage the floor.

The family decided to let the bear — which Schmaus's five-year-old daughter named Blue — stay through the winter until he was done hibernating and had moved on so they could board up the crawl space.

Noting that she couldn't do anything in the meantime to evict her uninvited tenant, Wing told the newspaper, "I should charge the bear rent."

PAWS FOR A NAP

A sleepy black bear wanting a comfy place to nap found exactly what he was looking for — in the screened-in back patio of an occupied house. And then, as startled family members hid inside, he took an hour-long snooze.

The hairy intruder had strolled out of the woods behind Alice MacDonough's home on a steamy summer day in 2013 in Naples, Florida. Wanting to catch a few z's in the shade, he tore through the screen of the family's lanai and plopped himself down on the cool tile floor.

Alice was not home, but her children, Mason and Preston, were inside with their babysitter, who made them get down on their hands and knees and crawl to a back bedroom for safety. However, when they realized that the bear was just yawning and scratching himself before getting some shut-eye, they ventured out of the room, but remained in the house.

"I couldn't believe my eyes," Mason told WBBH-TV. "It was so big."

"You don't really think when you see something like that," said Preston. "So we were all just freaking out."

Through the closed sliding-glass door, Preston took video of the sleeping bruin while Mason texted his mother. Here are the text messages the MacDonoughs shared with WBBH (complete with misspellings):

"Mom!! there's a bear in the lana not outside inside our porch help"

"!!!!"

"not jokin"

"Next too couch outside help!!!"

"He's sleeping"

"Sleeping that's right"

"The bear sleeping in the Lana"

"Inside the Lana"

"Omg"

"!"

"Sleeping omg"

"What do we do"

Alice rushed home to find the eight-foot bear still sprawled in the lanai, snoring away. She said the family had lived there for ten years and from time to time had seen black bears emerge from the nearby woods and roam around the family's backyard. She suspected that the bear might have been the same one that snatched pizza and Chinese takeout from her neighbor's patio earlier in the week.

Shortly before a team from the Florida Fish and Wildlife Conservation Commission arrived at the MacDonoughs, the bear had awakened and lumbered off into the woods.

A SWIMMINGLY GOOD TIME

When the temperatures soared into the triple digits on a summer day in 2012 in Pasadena, California, a mom let her two offspring play in the pool. There was nothing unusual about that, except it wasn't their pool and they weren't children. They were cubs.

With mama bear nearby, the two cubs jumped into the backyard pool of homeowner Maral Shekerdemian during a stiflingly hot afternoon. Once Shekerdemian recovered from her shock, she used her cell phone to film the bears swimming and playing with the pool's plastic vacuum line, which was floating on the surface.

"I saw two little cubs in my swimming pool, and they were just having a great time swimming and pulling the vacuum out and just having a blast like little kids," she told KCAL-TV.

After splashing around for 15 minutes, the cubs

got out of the pool and joined their mother in a nearby tree for an afternoon nap. They were the same bears that a neighbor had seen earlier, drinking from the sprinklers in her yard. The animals eventually climbed down the tree and returned to the nearby Angeles National Forest.

OVER-BEARING FOODIES

If a woman in a Siberian village was wondering if her soup was any good, she found the answer from an oversized critic — a bear that had barged onto her porch and slurped it all down.

According to the Russian news agency RIA Novosti, a woman had made a big pot of borscht — a hearty traditional soup of beets and meat — and left it on the front porch of her home in Ust-Ilimsk, Siberia, to cool off one autumn evening in 2013. She and her husband were going to eat it for supper.

But an uninvited guest spoiled their dinner plans. While they were taking a late afternoon nap in their home, they heard loud noises coming from outside. The couple peered out the window and saw a large bear prowling around the porch. They weren't too worried at first, until the bear caught a whiff of the borscht and headed for the pot of soup.

Not knowing what to do, they phoned the local community manager, who called the police. Meanwhile, the couple watched helplessly as the bear lapped up the tasty borscht. When the police arrived, they fired shots into the air to scare the soup slurper. He took off into the woods. The borscht must have been rated two paws up because the bear didn't leave a drop of soup for the couple.

Bears are supposed to eat nuts, berries, plants, and insects. But when two wild brown bears caught the aroma of steaming-hot homemade Chinese food wafting out a kitchen window, they smashed their way into a California house and devoured the meal.

Justin Lee, 25, of Monrovia, California, was getting ready to leave his upstairs bedroom one day in 2013 to sit down for lunch and enjoy a plate of home-cooked Chinese food that his mother had prepared and left on the table for him. Suddenly, his dog, Melo, a Maltese-poodle mix, began barking in alarm.

"He was at the staircase barking louder than I ever heard him bark before," Lee said to KTLA-TV. When Lee went downstairs to investigate, he saw the doggy door had been ripped out and the sliding-glass door leading to the backyard had been pried open. To his surprise, he came face-to-face with a bear. "I had a really awkward moment staring at the bear, super shocked, and then eventually the bear takes a few steps in . . . completely inside," Lee told KTLA. "We were just, like, locking eyes."

Lee grabbed Melo, dashed upstairs, barricaded himself in a room, and called 911. As he waited for police to arrive, he looked out his window, hoping the intruder had left. Instead, he saw a second bear, twice the size of the first one, in the back, heading for the house. Moments later, both animals were in the kitchen, knocking dishes to the ground and tipping the trash can as they scooped the food off the plates.

Lee knew why the bears made an unexpected visit: His mom's Chinese cooking. "She made the lunch and left," he said. "But the windows were open, and [the bears] just caught that scent."

After gobbling up the meal meant for Lee, the bears ate Melo's food, too. They left quite a mess in the kitchen. "The garbage was on the floor, our food was eaten," Lee told KTLA.

Monrovia police and animal-control officers waited for the bears to leave the house on their own. The officers used special soft bullets to scare the bears into the woods, but not before the bruins rolled around in the family's flower bed. Despite the intrusion, Lee said he didn't "bear" a grudge.

BEARERS OF BAD NEWS

Looking to break into television, a mama bear and her three cubs prevented the broadcast of a live weather forecast when they walked onto the set, scared the daylights out of the weatherman, and sent him scurrying for safety.

WNEP-TV in Scranton, Pennsylvania, uses an outdoor weather studio for the station's meteorologists to deliver their forecasts, barring severe weather. The set is a simple, foliage-covered area with a small man-made waterfall as its centerpiece.

One night in 2012, meteorologist Kurt Aaron was seconds away from doing his live forecast from the outdoor set, called the Backyard, when he heard a rustling in the bushes. When he saw bears emerge, he bolted for the inside of the station.

As viewers waited for the weather, a TV anchor broke in with the announcement, "We're told Kurt's not in the Backyard because there're bears outside?"

Studio cameras cut to the weather set that Aaron had just abandoned. In his place were the black bears, making their television debuts. They weren't doing anything extraordinary; just sniffing around the area.

From inside the station, Aaron, who seemed somewhat breathless from running, told his viewers, "They walked right up on me. I hear this sound, and I turn around and the bears are literally ten feet from me. And I ran like I stole something, I'm not gonna lie."

Meanwhile, the news anchors seemed fascinated by the bears as the cameras tracked the bruins for more than two minutes. When the cameras finally turned to Aaron, he gave his TV audience a shortened version of the weather.

The mama and her three cubs stuck around the set for more than half an hour before bidding their stardom good-bye.

"I had always been told it's best not to run [from a bear]," Aaron told the *Scranton Times-Tribune*. But he disregarded that advice when he realized he was "closer to the bear than I was to getting back to the building." He added, "I didn't realize how fast I could run for a 44-year-old guy."

This wasn't the first time WNEP's live weather forecasts had been interrupted by uninvited creatures.

Foxes, raccoons, and skunks have also starred in supporting roles during the station's weather reports.

DISORDER IN THE COURT

A black cat sent a courtroom into chaos when it tumbled out of a ceiling, disrupted a trial, sent people scrambling for the exits, and then charged the judge.

It all happened in 2012 during a trial of a suspected shoplifter in Gaborone, the capital of the African country of Botswana.

According to the Botswana weekly, the *Sun*, the feline plopped down from the ceiling — which was in disrepair — and landed with a loud bang in the public gallery. Although the cat was good-looking, it lost its appeal with many spectators and judicial workers who were superstitious about a black cat. There was no pussyfooting around. They immediately bolted out of the courtroom in fear.

For some reason, the cat then scampered toward magistrate Peggy Madandume, interrupting her. When the cat jumped onto the bench, Madandume ran for her life. Prosecutors and defense lawyers didn't judge her, because they had already taken cover. A courthouse guard tried to scare the cat away, but the intruder refused to leave. Instead, it jumped onto a case file that the magistrate was using at the time.

The court session had to be halted for more than 15 minutes while the cat had the entire courtroom to itself. Everyone else remained standing outside the complex, afraid to confront the fierce feline. Eventually, the cat had all the fun it could stand and quietly sauntered out of the courtroom as if nothing had happened.

Meanwhile, defendants who were in the courtroom when the cat dropped in had taken advantage of the bedlam by trying to escape. The police quickly rounded up all the accused.

Kgaodi Maleke, who witnessed the trying trial in the courtroom, told the *Africa Review* that the incident was alarming. "It's not funny, because we all know black cats are associated with witchcraft, so when such incidents happen, it's quite frightening."

While some people thought the cat was having a hiss-y fit, others thought it was just "kitten" around.

BREAKING BAD

When a dangerous animal escapes from the zoo, that's news. A black bear made similar news, but with a major twist — by breaking *into* the zoo.

One summer night in 2013, a bruin climbed a ten-foot-tall chain-link fence just to sneak inside the Knoxville (Tennessee) Zoo.

Rangers at the zoo were told that a 150-pound black bear was wandering around nearby in Chilhowee Park that evening. Around midnight, they spotted the animal climbing the tall, barbwire-topped perimeter fence and dropping inside the zoo. At first, they thought it might have been one of the attraction's bears that somehow had escaped from its compound for an evening stroll and was now trying to get back in before getting caught for breaking curfew. But a nose count of the resident bruins confirmed that all four were safely in their open-air enclosure and had not tried to sneak out.

Realizing the bear wasn't one of their own, staff members immediately began an intensive search of the zoo's 53 acres for the unauthorized visitor. Whether the bear broke into the zoo to see his friends or to spring them from their enclosure, no one knows. He was just as clever getting out as he was sneaking in because rangers never did find him. Convinced that the bear had left the way he came, the staff opened the zoo as scheduled.

Amy Flew, curator of mammals, said the area around Knoxville is bear country. She explained that the surprise visit came at a time of year when the younger bears are starting to seek out their own territory.

When asked why the bear broke into the zoo, executive director Lisa New told WBIR-TV that the zoo is a great attraction, "so maybe word has gotten out in the black bear community."

What's more bizarre than an animal breaking into a zoo? How about one that breaks into a *prison*.

Either a bobcat felt guilty about violating a law or else he was confused, because he sneaked into a prison — even though it houses some maximum-security units.

About 11:30 P.M. one night in 2012, the wild critter crept up to the Monroe Correctional Complex, located north of Seattle, Washington. The prison, which holds 2,400 inmates, is surrounded by fences fortified by razor wire. As officers were making their rounds along the perimeter, they spotted the bobcat between two tall cyclone fences inside the prison grounds. When the animal saw the guards, it took off. But rather than run into the woods, it ran through the razor wire and into the prison.

Bounding past the startled officers, the bobcat didn't bother to look for a hiding spot somewhere on the ground. Instead, the agile animal climbed onto the roof of the special offenders unit. In the wee hours of the morning, guards finally found it.

The prison staff called local veterinarian Roger Hancock, who shot the bobcat from about 40 feet away with a tranquilizer gun. Hancock then climbed a ladder, secured the unconscious animal with a noose on the end of a pole, and put it into a portable kennel. He transported the animal to the Pilchuck Veterinary Hospital in Snohomish, where it received stitches for deep cuts to a back paw and rear flank from running through the razor wire. When the young, 25-pound bobcat recovered, it was released back into the wild.

Although a bobcat breached the state's second-largest prison, officials said they weren't worried that an inmate could escape the same way. "If we had an inmate the same size as a bobcat with the same level of dexterity, then we'd be concerned," department of corrections spokesman Chad Lewis told KOMO-TV.

No one knows why the bobcat broke into the prison. "For whatever reason, I'm sure it was wondering, 'Where the heck am I?'" said prison spokeswoman Susan Biller.

VANDALS

FIRE DOG

When Yogi the dog starred in his first video, he created a firestorm of interest in more ways than one.

His owner, Hali Hudson, of Los Angeles, agreed to let Yogi, an eight-year-old Welsh corgi, appear in a 2012 video produced by the animal website The Pet Collective, a source for pet videos on the Internet, for its show "Pet Sense." Each episode focuses on a pet that needs help working through its odd issues. In Yogi's case, he has a thing about cleaning supplies and spray cans. The rambunctious dog attacks them with a vengeance every chance he gets.

No one can explain why he hates cleaning supplies. Hudson said the otherwise sweet dog has always been that way since she first adopted him when he was two months old. She told Yahoo News, "When he was younger, I'd yell at him to come back. He'd just ignore me. And then I'd grab the Lysol can, spray it, and he would come running back" because he wanted to bite it.

For the taping of the web show, Hudson opened the doors to her kitchen cabinet under the sink where her cleaning supplies were kept. With the camera rolling, Yogi charged into the cabinet and attacked the cans. In his excitement, he clamped down on a can of black spray paint and punctured it, causing black paint to spew out, splattering him and the white cabinets, appliances, and floor.

Yogi was unhurt and didn't seem to mind that black paint was covering his face. Hudson took Yogi off-camera to clean him up in the bathroom. Meanwhile, the camera kept rolling, showing the mess in the kitchen.

Suddenly, the fumes from the ruptured can mixed with the pilot light inside the gas stove, causing a small explosion and fireball that was caught on video. After a few shouts from the shocked crew members and Hudson, the fire was quickly put out. No one was hurt and damage was kept to a minimum.

"I heard the explosion and I felt it," Hudson said in a follow-up Pet Collective video. "If Yogi was still standing in that kitchen when that bomb exploded, he would have gone up in flames because he was covered in that paint. I don't even think [Yogi] was aware that he set my kitchen on fire."

Despite the explosion, Yogi still hasn't learned to curb his hatred for cleaning supplies. "Nothing has changed," Hudson told Yahoo News. "But I didn't really expect it to."

Hudson said she no longer keeps her cleaning supplies or spray paint under the sink anymore. But every time she opens the cabinet, Yogi still runs in there looking for those hated cans. Old habits die hard.

ATTACK ZONE

Dogs belonging to professional hockey player Karl Alzner, defenseman for the Washington Capitals, were apparently upset when his team lost to the New York Rangers in triple overtime in 2012.

When he came home from the deflating loss at 2 A.M., the exhausted player discovered that his three pets had trashed the living room. They had torn up magazines, scattering pieces all over the room. They had chewed on a teddy bear, slippers, and pillows. They had knocked over knickknacks.

Despite the late hour and still hurting from the crushing defeat, Alzner accepted the dogs' vandalism with good humor. He snapped a picture of two of them, Duncan and Charlie, who proudly posed in front of their destruction. Then he tweeted the picture, adding the caption, "Dogs not happy about the loss either."

Duncan, Charlie, and a third dog, Murphy, lived with Alzner and his fiancée, Mandy, in a townhouse. "Usually we have the dogs in a crate," the player told *NHL Live* hosts E.J. Hradek and Deb Placey. "But Mandy was leaving early to go to the game, and we knew that they'd be in [the crates] for a while."

Alzner felt sorry for his pets, so he decided to let them roam the house for the night. "We thought maybe we'll give them a chance," he said. "Everything should be fine."

But it wasn't. When Alzner and Mandy came back in the wee hours of the morning, "I was excited to be home and see the dogs," he said. The pooches greeted the couple at the front door, which was on the lower level of the townhouse. Without going up to the living room, which was on the second floor, Alzner and Mandy took the dogs outside for a quick walk. After they returned, they headed for the living room.

"We walked up the stairs and sure enough, there was their mess," Alzner told *NHL Live*. He was surprised by the destruction. It was obviously the last thing he wanted to see that night, especially after such a tough loss. Trying to make the best of a bad situation, Alzner took the picture of the culprits and tweeted it. The photo went viral.

"In the picture on the left is Duncan and on the right is Charlie," Alzner said on the show. "Another culprit is Murphy, who Mandy and I assume is the ringleader. He was hiding at the time."

The dogs were put back in the penalty box . . . er . . . cage.

CAR BATTERY

A bear broke into a car, became trapped, and then trashed the inside, causing a whopping $17,000 in damages.

In the middle of the night in 2013, the furry vandal — a huge 300-pound black bear — opened the unlocked Toyota Matrix owned by Heather Bybee, of Paisley, Florida, a small town near Orlando.

Bybee's father, Randy Moon, who shares the house with her and her two small children, told WFTV-TV that he woke up around 2:30 A.M. when he heard a strange noise. "I looked outside at the car and saw the dash light on," he said. "There was a bear tearing it all to pieces, going from side to side."

Moon grabbed the car keys to unlock the car door for the bear, who was not happy at all about being trapped inside for a few hours. "I stood there and opened the door," Moon told the TV station. "The bear and I were face-to-face. I said, 'You gotta get out of here.' He was foaming in the mouth."

Moon said he backed away immediately after opening the door. "I didn't want to be his dinner. When the bear got out, he was in double overdrive and ran into the woods."

The damage it left behind was astounding. The bear chewed off the driver's seat and part of the passenger's seat and left bite marks and claw marks all over the door panels. The trapped animal clawed through the interior roof, exposing the insulation inside, and it ripped apart the car's consoles, scattering pieces all over the floor.

Black bears often roam the neighborhood in rural Lake County, which borders the Ocala National Forest, but Bybee never expected one would get into her car and destroy the interior.

"I guess I didn't lock it up," she told the *Orlando Sentinel*. "But there's nothing in the car for the bear to want."

Judging from all the paw prints on the car, Bybee and Moon think the bear was trying to climb onto the roof of the car and got its back paw stuck on the door handle, opening the door. The curious bear then climbed into the car, looking for something to eat or steal. Because of the bruin's weight, the car began rocking, causing the door to close and trap the animal inside. In its anger and frustration, it tore up the interior trying to escape.

Bybee said this wasn't the first time that the family had bear trouble. She said they used to have a 30-pound pig in the yard, but a bear took off with the little porker, which was never seen again. Earlier, a bear had broken into their shed and another one tried to get into her father's pickup truck, but couldn't because the doors were locked. The family often sees the bruins picking through the garbage.

Moon told WFTV that the car, which he helped his daughter buy four months earlier, was totaled. But

Bybee had problems getting the insurance company to pay for the destruction. "There was no [police] report to write up about a bear eating your car," she said.

When a TV reporter asked Bybee's preschool son, Donny, what he thought about the bear, the little boy replied, "He's a bully of cars."

CAR NUT

A Florida family was convinced that one of their cars was being vandalized by someone who had a grudge against them. They finally caught the culprit in the act, leaving them in complete surprise. The offender was a nutty squirrel.

One morning in 2013, Nora Ziegler, of Stuart, Florida, walked outside and noticed that her Toyota Sequoia had been damaged. It looked as if a six-inch hole had been cut out above the SUV's left front wheel well.

She called Martin County sheriff's deputies, who came out to investigate. "They asked me if I had any enemies, and I said no," she told WPTV-TV.

Later that day, Ziegler found another hole on the vehicle. This one was slightly larger than the first and was located above the left, rear wheel well. Once again, the deputies came out. After studying the odd destruction, they shook their heads and told the family they had never seen anything like that before.

"The police told me someone is coming after me," Nora told WPTV. It was an unsettling thought for her and her family. They wondered why, with five cars outside, only her SUV had been targeted, and in such a strange manner.

They finally got their answers later in the day when Ziegler was taking out the garbage and she spotted the vandal in action — a crazy squirrel with a taste for cars. Hoping to get incriminating evidence against the criminal, she took out her smartphone and began shooting video of the squirrel chomping on the car. When the squirrel saw it was being filmed, it scampered off.

Hugh Curran, with Absolute Critter Removal of Port St. Lucie, told WPTV that squirrels have been known to chew through car wires, but it was strange that this particular one would try eating the car itself. However, he added, it's not unusual for a squirrel to chew through things looking to find a cavity to make a nest.

"I'm not happy to see my car like this, but at least I didn't have any enemies — at least not people," Ziegler told the TV station. The family decided to give the squirrel a nickname: Munchy.

Phoenix the pet cockatoo had his own sense of fashion when he altered — well, actually ruined — an expensive evening gown just days before his owner planned to wear it to one of New York City's most glamorous events.

The snow-white bird was a Christmas gift in 2010 from New York governor Andrew Cuomo to girlfriend Sandra Lee, a popular host of the Food Network. The bird quickly won the celebrity chef's heart.

"Having a cockatoo is almost like having a dog," Lee told *People* magazine in 2012. "He follows me around on foot. He sits on my lap as we watch TV, and he cuddles constantly. I am a true animal person, and I'm stunned by how engaged, alert, and connected he is to his world. He's an absolute joy and a pleasure, and he has become a real focus in my life."

Her feathered friend was anything but a joy and a pleasure in 2013 after he managed to sneak into her huge walk-in closet, which was filled with pricey designer clothes. Without Lee aware of what he was doing, Phoenix hopped onto a one-of-a-kind, floor-length, black, beaded evening gown.

Lee had her heart set on wearing the expensive dress to the annual Costume Institute Gala — fashion's biggest event of the year — at the Metropolitan Museum of Art. Everyone who was anyone in New York would be there in their finery, showing off their elegant gowns and classy evening wear. Lee was looking forward to walking the red carpet in a dress made exclusively for her by fashion designer Vivienne Westwood.

Lee never got the chance, not after Phoenix had altered it.

Just four days before the posh Met Gala, Lee pulled the gown off its special hanger in the closet and screamed with alarm. "Phoenix had severed nearly every bead, crystal, and pearl from the dress," she told the *New York Times*. "No joke. Two weeks before, I had received my invitation to the Met Gala excited about this year's theme . . . I had a Vivienne Westwood dress . . . perfect for the Gala."

Except it was no longer perfect — or wearable, for that matter — after what Phoenix had done to it.

Lee didn't say if she punished the birdbrain. After failing to find a suitable alternative during a hasty shopping spree, Lee "settled" for a designer dress that she had worn at a birthday party for rock star Elton John.

CAMERA SHY

An elephant that didn't want his picture taken made sure to let his feelings be known — by tossing around thousands of dollars' worth of camera equipment.

Nature photographer Paul Souders, 52, of Seattle, Washington, wanted to take some close-ups of a herd of male elephants in Chobe National Park in the African nation of Botswana. He planted remote-controlled cameras at the edge of watering holes, hoping to get some amazing close-ups of the giant animals. From the safety of a truck 30 to 50 yards away, the photographer could snap his pictures.

Souders got some remarkable shots, but they weren't exactly what he had in mind. That's because one seven-ton bull elephant was in no mood for pictures — and his opinion carried a lot of weight. When the big beast saw the cameras at one of his favorite spots, he became angry and began knocking and throwing the equipment into a mudhole.

One of the photos that Souders took shows the elephant examining a camera on a small tripod. Then the animal picks it up with its trunk and tosses it into the mud.

"Elephants are intelligent and curious creatures, so I wasn't surprised that he inspected the camera with his trunk, sniffing at it delicately," Souders told London's *Daily Mail*. "But the utter contempt and disdain when he picked it up and gave it a toss, that hurt my feelings a little. If I had to guess, he was merely annoyed that there was this silly, clicky thing in the way of where he wanted to drink."

Souders, who also placed cameras in Nxai Pan National Park and along the Botete River in Makgadikgadi Pans National Park, discovered that elephants there weren't too happy about his gear, either, and knocked them over, too, while drinking water. They obviously were "multi-tusking." The cameras were worth from $650 to $6,500 apiece.

"There might be someone crazy enough to lie down in a mud pool and try to photograph elephants from five feet away, but I'm not that guy anymore," Souders told the newspaper. "I put the cameras out there and let them take the risks. You just have to be willing to watch it get destroyed."

Souders, who was able to retrieve his damaged cameras and get them repaired, added, "Next time I try this, I will plan a little better and protect my cameras in waterproof cases."

BABOON GOONS

A roving gang of baboons in a South African resort town climbed through an open upstairs window and ransacked the place — and it was all caught on video.

One day in 2013 in the town of Betty's Bay, the monkey troop entered the open window of a house of a person who was away. Seeing the break-in, neighbor Howard James Fyvie grabbed his video camera and, with two of his friends, went to investigate.

They peered through the windows and saw that the animals were trashing the place. The baboons raced around the house, knocking over lamps, breaking dishes, yanking items out of drawers and cabinets, raiding the refrigerator, and scouring the cupboards. Many of them were eating leftover fried chicken and ripping open containers of food.

While recording the baboons running amok, Fyvie and his friends went into the house to oust the vandals. Seeing the humans, some of the baboons fled out the open window. Others had to be chased around the house with a broom. Yelling at the baboons to leave, the men used a small ladder to prod some of the reluctant ones out the window.

One stubborn baboon remained in an upstairs bathroom, trying to open a cabinet.

Brandishing the broom, Fyvie yelled, "Get out of here! Here's the door!" The baboon wasn't intimidated and angrily barked at Fyvie, who made a hasty retreat. Eventually, the last primate left the house and was last seen escaping over a garden wall.

BAAAAAD GOATS

Goats have been known to climb onto the roofs of barns and sheds. But a dozen young ones in a village in India chose the wrong thing to jump on — a brand-new police car. Their antics caused major damage to the vehicle, leading to the arrest of three of them.

No "kid"-ding.

Police in Kilpauk, a rural area of the city of Chennai, had just taken possession of a new maroon Toyota Innova for their department in 2013. It was parked in front of the police station right next to a field where the 12 goats were grazing.

In hindsight, that was probably a mistake, because the police had already received reports that these particular goats had a habit of wandering away and climbing onto cars and trucks of residents and shopkeepers, scratching and denting the vehicles.

Why the goats loved to jump on cars and trucks is

anyone's guess. A dozen of them took turns climbing onto the shiny, new Toyota. They were having a good time until someone alerted the cops inside the station that their squad car was being used as a prop for the goats' version of "king of the hill."

Police rushed outside, chased off the goats, and then stared with dismay at the new vehicle, which now looked as if it had just come from a demolition derby. The hood and roof were dented, the body paint was scratched, the windshield was cracked, and the wipers were broken.

"The goats crossed the line," an officer told the *Times of India*. "We got the vehicle two days ago."

The cops managed to capture three of the vandals and took them into custody. When police learned the goats' owner was Mary Arogynathan, 37, a resident of Shastry Nagar, she was charged with negligence for failure to keep her animals properly penned. Meanwhile, the four-legged vandals were being held by authorities as "scapegoats."

NOT SO FUNNY BUNNY BUSINESS

Rabbits have been vandalizing cars parked at Denver International Airport (DIA) and people are hopping mad about it.

For years, reports have surfaced of rabbits eating spark plug cables, brake lines, and other wiring of cars in the parking lots at DIA, causing thousands of dollars in damage. Although the actual number of cases is small compared to the average number of vehicles that are parked there every day (more than 10,000), the furry vandals are still creating problems for a few unlucky drivers.

Dexter Meyer, of Stapleton, Colorado, had a "bad hare" day after he returned from a nine-day vacation and went to start his new Volkswagen Jetta that he had left at the DIA parking lot. "I turned on the ignition, and all these lights started flashing," he told KUSA-TV. "I pulled out the manual, and it said I had a big problem, so I took it back to the dealership. The service manager said, 'You didn't have the car parked at DIA, did you?' And I said, 'Actually, yes, that's where I picked the car up.' And he said, 'We've had a significant number of problems with rabbits eating through the wiring in people's cars.'" Meyer spent $238 to have his vehicle fixed.

Ken Blum told KCNC-TV that he needed repairs done twice on his car at a total cost of $700 because of hungry hares at the DIA parking lot. "When I had the trouble with the oil light coming on, the dealer told me the wires that controlled the air-conditioning were chewed," Blum said.

Airport shuttle driver Michelle Anderson told KCNC in 2013, "I see at least dozens [of rabbits] every morning. They go hide under the cars, and the cars are warm."

Arapahoe Autotek spokesman Wiley Faris told the TV station that the rabbits like to chew on the insulator portion of the ignition cables. "That's what we see most," he said. Faris added that one effective way to stop the rabbits from chewing on the cables is to coat the wires with the urine of a fox or a coyote. "We have found a good deterrent is predator urine," he said. "You can pick up fox urine at any pro hunting shop."

The harmful hares are not just a problem at DIA. Private parking lots near the airport have reported similar troubles.

DIA and City of Denver officials say any repairs needed from damage caused by the rabbits are the responsibility of the driver. Unfortunately, most insurance companies won't cover the costs.

But the bunnies might be living on "burrowed" time, because the airport has instituted several measures to prevent the undercarriage sabotage. Wildlife experts have built perches around the parking lot for hawks and eagles to more easily spot and prey on the rabbits. New fences have been installed to prevent the hares from digging under them. And United States Department of Agriculture Wildlife Services agents patrol the parking lots, removing an average of one hundred rabbits a month.

Eventually, officials hope they can tell the rabbits, "It's been nice 'gnawing' you."

FIREPLUG

A family cat caused the fire department to show up at a residence — for peeing.

In 2012 in New Castle, Pennsylvania, a worker for Columbia Gas was at the house, checking for a possible gas leak when he noticed that an electrical outlet was smoking. He called 911.

Firefighters responded immediately and discovered that where there's smoke, there isn't necessarily fire. They determined that the cat had peed on an electrical outlet on the floor, and the urine had caused the receptacle to smoke. They shut off the power to that circuit, and the owner cleaned up the mess.

It's not known whether the owner told the cat, "Urine so much trouble!"

OH, DEER!

A doe shattered a window to get into a bank, apparently looking for some bucks.

The deer busted into a PNC Bank in Oakdale, Pennsylvania, one morning in 2012 by crashing through a window. "We thought someone broke into the bank," employee Maree Campbell told KDKA-TV. "It was a deer."

Once inside, the intruder froze, not sure what to do next. "It was actually staring toward the vault," Campbell said.

While the deer wasn't in any hurry to leave, employees called authorities. "We were hoping they weren't going to shoot it," Campbell said. "Maybe tranquilize it." But that wasn't necessary. They simply shooed the animal — which didn't appear to be injured — out the back door. The "deerly"-departed animal then hightailed it into the nearby woods.

A similar break-in occurred six years earlier in the Pittsburgh area when a buck smashed the front glass window of the office of Mellon Financial in Fox Chapel.

Officer Cheryl Watson told KDKA, "We got a call that there was a burglar alarm at Mellon Bank. By the time I arrived, I saw that a window had been broken and the deer was inside."

The buck stopped there. Police came up with a game plan and tried to lure the animal outside with some sweet rolls, but it was too terrified to leave. An animal control officer arrived and prodded the intruder to leave through the large busted window.

Branch manager Michael Babjak told KDKA, "He leaped over a desk, knocked over some pencils and [a] coffeepot, and went out the broken window. I can't believe the deer could crash through a window that thick. The deer didn't appear to be injured."

It ran out so fast that, in hindsight, it looked like watching a deer fly.

BAD BOYS

GETTING HIS GOAT

A pet goat named Voldemort knocked a paperboy off his bike, chased him up a tree, and held him hostage for an hour.

Jaxon Gessel, 14, was on his bicycle delivering newspapers in the predawn hours in 2012 in the small town of Smithfield, Utah, when the bizarre mugging occurred.

Voldemort, an otherwise friendly black goat, had broken free from his chain at the home of his owner. The goat walked across Main Street and then spotted Jaxon. In the darkness, the boy thought, at first, the goat was a dog and didn't pay any attention to it. But then Voldemort started making a grunting noise, charged after Jaxon, and headbutted him off his bike. The boy tried to get back on his bike to escape, but the goat knocked him down again.

"It just freaked me out when it stood up on its hind legs and, like, wrapped its front legs around me and pulled me off," Jaxon told KSL-TV. He said he scrambled to his feet and climbed a nearby tree for safety. The goat wouldn't leave and just kept staring at the boy for an hour.

The standoff finally ended when Voldemort saw new potential targets — two little girls walking to school — and began chasing them. They ran, screaming. Jaxon then jumped down from the tree, caught up to the goat about two blocks away, and grabbed Voldemort's collar.

Meanwhile, Smithfield police were searching for Jaxon after receiving a call from his parents, who said he was long overdue from his paper route. During the search, police got another call from a resident reporting that a boy was struggling with a goat.

When police officer Brandon Muir arrived on the scene, the thuggish goat suddenly acted more like a happy puppy. Muir said Voldemort was overly friendly.

"It jumped on me a few times," he told the newspaper. "But he wasn't that hard to catch."

The officer also noticed that Jaxon's bag, which held the newspapers, was still up in the tree where the boy had been perched earlier.

The goat was impounded by Smithfield animal control officers, but was later returned home. Named after the villain of the popular Harry Potter series, Voldemort had not been in trouble before, Marissa Benson, his owner, told KSL. "He's a really good pet, good with kids, a good lawnmower," she said.

Ironically, had Jaxon known what kind of goat Voldemort was, he might not have ended up in a tree. The animal was a fainting goat — the kind that topples over when frightened. Had Jaxon scared him instead of the other way around, the goat would have fallen to the ground and remained motionless for at least ten seconds.

Jaxon said it was one of the strangest mornings of his life. "People are just like, 'Why are you scared of goats?' I'm like, 'That was a freaky goat. I think it's possessed or something.'"

When word spread in school about his encounter, Jaxon ended up with a new nickname. Friends began kidding him by calling him "Goat Boy."

HOW DAIRY YOU?

A roving gang of cows crashed a small party of recent college graduates and bullied them for their beer.

Kevin Spencer was hosting a party for his daughter, Lauren, and about a dozen of her fellow grads in the backyard of his house in Boxford, Massachusetts, in 2012 when six cows — all uninvited — showed up. The intruders were in no "moo'ed" to leave, at least not until the cops showed up.

Earlier in the evening, the six-month-old, black-and-white 500-pound cows had knocked down a fence in search of greener pastures. "They came a quarter mile down the road, heard the music, and saw the lights and a fire," Spencer told WHDH-TV. "They decided it was cows' night out, and they wanted to drink."

As they ambled down the road, they stopped at neighbors' houses. In a 911 call, one person told the dispatcher, "We thought they were deer, but they're huge, huge, huge cows! There's got to be five or six of them!"

Another call came from Andrea Poritzky: "I just went downstairs, and I have six cows in my yard. I don't own cows."

Wondering what the beef was about, Lieutenant James Riter responded to the call and saw the cows in the front yard of the Spencer residence. Spotting the cop, the leader of the bovines steered them to the backyard.

Riter told WHDH that after the herd went to the rear of the house, "I could hear them [the girls] screaming in the backyard, and I hoped they weren't getting trampled."

He ran behind the house and saw an "udderly" ridiculous sight: The cows had chased off the young women and were now drinking from the plastic cups and cans of beer that had been left on a picnic table.

"The cows just went in and helped themselves," Riter said. "They [the partygoers] got up as the cows went toward the table. The girls stepped back, and the cows took over the table, knocking over the beers with their noses and drinking the beer off the table. I saw one cow drinking the beer on its way down as it spilled off the table."

The cows were milking this opportunity for all it was worth. They even started rooting around the recycling bin, looking for some extra drops of beer in discarded cans and cups.

Spencer was inside the house and unaware of the unwelcome visitors. He said his daughter rushed up to him to tell him about the party crashers. At first, he thought she was either joking or had too much to drink.

"She said, 'Dad, there are cows outside!' And I said, 'That's it. The party's over.'"

When he went to investigate, he was "amoosed" to see the cows. "They were having a good time," Spencer said.

But the cows' owner, Pat Canonica, arrived and put an end to the bovines' "unreason-a-bull" behavior. They were given a police escort — a squad car in front and one in the rear — back to their own pasture.

KUNG FU KANGAROO

A rather mean kangaroo got a kick out of roughing up an Australian politician.

The roo was grazing on the front lawn of a suburban house in the capital city of Canberra when it mugged Shane Rattenbury, 41, a minister in the Australian Capital Territory government, who was out for a morning jog one day in May 2013.

The runner had just passed a tall hedge when the kangaroo sprang into action and ambushed him. "I didn't see the kangaroo, and it didn't see me," Rattenbury told CNN.com. "It started hopping around and was a bit panicked. I ducked for cover. The kangaroo jumped on me in its attempt to get away, and I ended up on the ground. We both got a nasty fright, and of course when kangaroos are startled, they lash out."

Rattenbury said the four-foot, seven-inch eastern grey kangaroo had knocked him to the sidewalk. The claws of the animal's powerful hind legs dug deeply into the back of the politician's left leg, drawing blood. The animal then bounded off toward a nearby nature reserve, leaving Rattenbury lying dazed and bleeding in the street.

Eastern grey kangaroos are common in the suburbs of Canberra, especially during May, when the dry weather brings them searching for grass and water on people's lawns.

"I see kangaroos here all the time when I'm running," Rattenbury said. But, he added, he never had one that actually crashed into him before.

The victim went to an urgent-care center where his wounds were cleaned and bandaged and he was given a tetanus shot.

To his followers on Twitter, he tweeted, "I believe the roo is fine — escaped the scene quickly, but did fail to get my watch or wallet, for those who were wondering."

Three hours after the mugging, Rattenbury limped into the Australian Capital Territory Legislative Assembly, where some of his colleagues ribbed him about the ambush. "There have certainly been a lot of kangaroo jokes and kangaroo puns in the parliament," he said. Someone told him he should get a "hop-eration." Another one suggested that if Rattenbury had acted like a joey (a baby kangaroo), he could have ended up as a "pouch potato."

STRONG-ARM TACTICS

An octopus snatched an expensive camera from a snorkeler and filmed itself during a wild, five-minute underwater chase off the coast of New Zealand.

In 2010, videographer Victor Huang, of San Francisco, was snorkeling in the clear waters near the city of Wellington. Carrying a new $700 underwater video camera and a speargun, Huang was swimming about nine feet below the surface when he was mugged by the eight-armed bandit.

"Out of nowhere, the octopus dashes out of the seaweed and grabs a hold of me," he recalled for Harry Smith, then host of CBS's *The Early Show*. "I was initially freaked-out, because I was free diving three meters underwater on a breath hold."

Huang admitted he briefly panicked while trying to unwrap the tentacles from around his wrist. The octopus, which had an arm span of about five feet, was apparently attracted to the snorkeler's shiny video camera and began prying open Huang's fingers to steal it. During the struggle, which was being recorded, the octopus yanked the camera from Huang's grip. "As soon as the octopus got it, it swam away really quickly, and I chased after it," he said.

Huang returned to the surface for air and then, while swimming, pursued the mugger for about five minutes. "It went into stealth mode and went into the rocks and tried to camouflage itself, and I saw my chance to get down toward it," he recalled.

Diving to the octopus, which had the recording camera in its mouth, Huang gently lifted the thief away from the rocks with his speargun. The octopus then wrapped its tentacles around the speargun and wouldn't let go.

Even though he knew the sea creature had a beak strong enough to crack a rock, Huang reached into its mouth and pried the camera free. "I figured the camera had some amazing footage so I took the risk and went for it," he told Smith.

Huang assumed the thief wanted the camera for its octopus garden. "The camera itself is sort of bright blue and metallic and shiny, and I think it just saw something a bit different and unique and wanted to collect it for its little gypsy collection," he said.

Having lost the camera, the octopus wouldn't let go of the speargun for several minutes even after Huang kept shaking it. Huang figured the animal just wanted to play. "I honestly felt completely safe with the octopus," he said. "If I didn't have to get to work at 9 A.M., I would have stayed out with it for hours just to sort of hang out with it."

Huang posted the octopus's video on YouTube, which has been seen by more than six million viewers.

SEAL OF DISAPPROVAL

A giant bull seal climbed into an inflatable dinghy and refused to budge, stranding a newly married couple on a remote island for four days.

The seal didn't care that the boat was the only way for Eddie Stebbings, 35, and his new wife, Bee Bueche, 36, to leave uninhabited Skomer Island, located three miles off the Pembrokeshire coast of Wales. The animal was bigger and more ornery than the humans, so he, and he alone, decided when he would leave.

Fortunately for the stuck couple, they were prepared, because they were wildlife wardens on the windswept island, home to more than 400 Atlantic grey seals. Stebbings and Bueche had chosen to spend their honeymoon on one of the United Kingdom's most remote islands. Skomer, managed by the Wildlife Trust of South and West Wales, is one of Britain's most important island bird sanctuaries.

As wardens, the main job of the husband and wife team was to study seals and to assist any newborns during seal pupping season in 2013. The couple used an inflatable dinghy to get their supplies. But when the giant lug took possession of the boat, they were sealed off from the mainland.

"One morning in October the seal flopped itself into the boat," Stebbings told London's *Daily Telegraph*. "It refused to budge for four days and was at one point joined by another seal. He was about four times my weight, eight feet long, and clearly not worried about people coming close to him."

No amount of cajoling or persuasion could oust the seal. There was nothing for the couple to do but wait him out.

Meanwhile, they continued their work of studying the seals and occasionally helping with the newborns. Stebbings had to rappel down 200-foot-high cliffs to mark the pups with a special waterproof dye to identify them. He rescued one pup from a cave after the young mammal had become trapped on a ledge. The couple also assisted pups that were born on the pebble beach and in the island's caves.

But the bull seal that took over their boat didn't care about all their good work. He just lounged for days in the dinghy until he grew bored. Then he left. So why did he commandeer the couple's boat? He wouldn't tell. His lips were "sealed."

TAKING THE BULL BY THE HORNS

An escapee from a ranch found out that the police in Fresno, California, don't tolerate any bull — even if it is one.

During rush hour one day in 2012, a big, brown 1,500-pound bull went on the loose in the southwestern section of the city, scaring neighbors and causing two elementary schools to go on lockdown for the students' safety. Although police hadn't received any reports that a bull had gone missing, 911 calls started rolling in about 8:30 A.M. of the beast trotting down the streets of Fresno.

"This is not an ordinary occurrence by any stretch," police lieutenant Burke Farrah told the *Los Angeles Times*.

"We're a city of a half million people, despite our reputation as a cow town."

Police weren't sure exactly what to do until a dispatcher remembered that motorcycle officer Tom Hardin Sr., who was at the station, had 30 years of ranch-roping experience. So Hardin was assigned the task of rounding up the runaway beast. "He's an excellent motorcycle cop as well as horseman," Farrah said.

Hardin hopped on his metal "steed" and took off after the bull, which was running at speeds of up to 15 miles per hour. Other police cars followed the animal in one of the city's oddest chases.

Rosemary Valenzuela told the newspaper she was in her driveway leaving for work when she saw police cars and motorcycles. "I thought it was a parade with all their lights flashing," she said. "Then I hear them say, 'Get in your house! Get in your vehicle!' And this big old thing comes whomp, whomp, whomping past into our backyard."

Hardin tried to herd the bull to a safe area, but the animal kept turning onto one street after another for nearly three miles. During the pursuit, it looked as though the bull had been cornered, and a trailer was brought in. Not too happy about being chased for all those blocks, the bull was in no mood to follow orders from the cops.

"He would charge my motorcycle," Hardin told KMPH-TV. "He reached up and kicked the bike."

Farrah said he was impressed with Hardin. "He stayed on his mount even after the bull kicked the motorcycle."

At one point, the bull appeared to give up. He hopped into the trailer and then thought better of it. He jumped right out and took off again. "Unfortunately a fifteen-hundred-pound bull has a mind of its own, and it chose to walk through several neighborhoods in southwest Fresno, including an apartment complex," said Farrah.

When Yesenia Ochoa heard a commotion outside her home, she looked through her kitchen window and couldn't believe what she saw in the backyard. "It was an actual bull," she told the TV station. "It was mad and it ran through our fence in the back. It was just ramming through here mad."

She told the newspaper that from the safety of her house she watched Hardin take charge with the help of two other officers. "He was in a cop uniform on a motorcycle, but he had a rope over his head like a cowboy," she said.

The bull put his head down and started pawing, but Hardin refused to be intimidated. "The bull appeared he was going to charge," the officer told the TV station. "He got down low, started pawing the ground, and looked straight at me. So I swung the rope at him and lucky for us he decided to go the other way. He turned and went right in the trailer." This time he stayed, and they were able to secure the trailer.

Because the bull wasn't branded, police didn't know who it belonged to, so the animal was taken to a nearby stockyard until the owner was identified.

PICNIC PANIC

A hooligan of an alligator was looking for a bite to eat, so it emerged from the water, scared a group of picnickers, and ate all their hamburgers.

Rodney Cammauf, 68, of Pensacola, Florida, and some friends selected a spot at the edge of a waterway in Homestead, Florida, for an afternoon picnic in 2013. They put their food — burgers, chips, and soft drinks — on a bright-red plastic cloth on the ground.

Just when they were ready to eat, they were startled by a large gator that swam over to them. They backed away when the scaly thug came out of the water. But the gator wasn't interested in eating them. It was interested in their picnic food and made snappy work of the burgers.

While it was chomping on their meal, Cammauf cautiously crept closer and began taking photographs of the brute. "I felt extremely apprehensive when I saw the alligator approaching," he told reporters later. "They're obviously not fluffy rabbits, so you need to be very careful with them.

"In this particular location, alligators are used to seeing people, and many people often throw food into the water, so the gators have a taste for it now. I guess he just thought the picnic had been set up for him.

"In the end, the gator was chased back into the water by someone with a bit more experience. But, sadly, we lost all of our food. It's certainly an experience I won't forget. It's a warning to other people to watch where they set up their picnic in the future."

INSTI-GATOR

A cold-blooded thug menaced customers trying to use the front door of a Walmart in Florida.

The wrongdoer was a six-foot alligator that sauntered over to a Walmart in Apopka, Florida, and blocked the entryway, causing the automatic doors to open and close repeatedly. The big gator acted as if it dared anyone to get past it. No one did.

Employees prevented the scaly ruffian from entering or further setting off the sliding-glass doors by eventually locking them. Customers were directed away from the front and told to use a different entrance.

Meanwhile, Apopka police officers arrived and cordoned off the area. Despite the presence of the gator, most customers continued to do their shopping while others stayed outside, watching the reptile and taking photographs of it.

Customer Robin Watkins told WKMG-TV, "It was neat to see, but I'm glad they locked the doors for safety."

Police called a wildlife expert to trap the animal, but the brute crawled away and plopped into a nearby swampy area before it could be caught.

ROAD RAGE

A troop of baboons terrorized motorists on a major highway in and out of Cape Town, South Africa, by throwing rocks at passing cars.

The hairy thugs' road rage was at its peak in 1996 and 1997.

According to the *Pretoria News*, the N1 highway was only a stone's throw away from a gang of surly baboons who were ticked off by the constant din of Christmas holiday traffic in 1996. The offenders first attacked drivers outside the town of De Doorns by hurling stones at them as they drove by.

After the holidays, the baboons struck again. Principal traffic officer Kenny Africa told the newspaper that motorists were pelted with stones from the mountain slopes above the Protea Park Hotel. There were no reports of serious damage to cars or of injuries to motorists. Africa said that Inspector Danny Appolis, of the provincial traffic authority, stopped the stone hurlers by giving them a taste of their own medicine. He flung small rocks at the baboons until they fled from his one-man onslaught.

"At first the baboons were playing and throwing stones at each other," Africa told the newspaper. "Then they started throwing stones on the road." Soon the rock chucking escalated, targeting motorists. "Appolis arrived on the scene and threw several stones, forcing them to back off," Africa said.

By 2010 the devious troublemakers had come up with a clever scheme to harass tourists who got out of their vehicles to marvel at the oceanfront view from South Africa's Cape Peninsula.

If the baboons didn't hear the telltale "tweet" of a car's remote locking system, the ruffians would sneak over to the vehicle and open its door. Then they would plunder its contents and vandalize the interior while the unsuspecting owner was admiring the vista.

"The baboons are so intelligent," Theuns Vivian, destination development manager for Cape Town, told London's *Daily Telegraph*. "They're waiting for the sound of the car alarm being set. If they don't hear it, they think, 'Well, that door isn't locked.'"

When the tourists return to their car, they find it has been raided. The food for their picnics is taken and the inside of their vehicle is trashed. Sometimes, drivers who stop by the side of the road find themselves at the wrong place at the wrong time as roving bands of baboons descend on the car and damage it.

Signs around the area now warn visitors about the dangers of getting too close to the thugs. "These are dangerous animals, and you still have people trying to pose for a photograph next to a baboon with fangs the size of a cheetah's," Vivian said.

Apparently it's hard for tourists to understand that

baboons can't think straight when they have crooked thoughts.

BOTTLE-LY HARM

Hundreds of wild baboons were getting drunk and disorderly after feasting on grapes grown in the vineyards outside Cape Town, South Africa.

Baboons have raided vineyards for years, but farmers reported that 2010 was the worst year ever. One of the big reasons was that the primates lost their usual foraging areas because of wildfires.

To the whining of the region's winemakers, the ruffians had developed a discerning palate (in other words, a sensitive taste) for the most expensive grapes — the ones that are turned into kinds of wine known as Pinot Noir and Sauvignon Blanc. "They eat the sweetest ones and leave the rest," Francois van Vuuren, farm manager at La Terra de Luc vineyards, told London's *Daily Telegraph*.

The baboons' taste for wine had been costly for the winemakers. Out of a 12-ton harvest at La Terra de Luc in 2010, the baboons stripped more than a half ton of the grapes from the vine. In the Constantia region, La Petite Ferme had its annual production of 12 to 15 barrels of

Chardonnay reduced to only three barrels because of the baboons' raids on the vineyard, according to the newspaper.

Many of the invaders were having too much of a grape . . . er . . . great time because they got drunk after feasting on discarded grape skins that fermented in the sun. Winemakers often found the animals stumbling around in a drunken stupor or sleeping it off under a shady spot. Other trespassers were passed out on the ground.

Electric fences don't always work, because the clever baboons have sneaked into the vineyards by either digging underneath the fences or swinging over them from trees. Justin O'Riain, of the University of Cape Town, told the *Daily Telegraph* (Australia) that the baboons would test electric fences for weak spots. "If they're shocked, they'll scream, but they'll likely return the next day," he said. For the baboons, the risk is worth the reward because the succulent grapes are an "absolute bonanza," he added.

Some winemakers have had good luck using rubber snakes to scare off the baboons. Other vineyards have planted grapes *outside* their fence line, hoping that the baboons would eat those and ignore the more expensive grapes that are growing inside the fence.

Vineyards have employed guards with special sticks that give off a loud bang to frighten the trespassers. The guards have also tried to annoy them by blowing vuvuzelas, the plastic horns that fans blare at World Cup soccer matches.

"The baboons are not just eating our grapes, they are raiding our kitchens and ripping the thatch off the roofs," Jean Naude, general manager of the Groot Constantia winery, told the newspaper. "They are becoming increasingly bold and destructive."

A 12-year-old boy was left traumatized after confronting a troop that had broken into his house at a vineyard. According to the newspaper, he heard noises in the kitchen and went to investigate. There, he found the primates rummaging through the cupboards. Rather than flee when they saw him, three male baboons chased the boy upstairs and surrounded him. While he called for help on the phone, the animals pelted him with fruit.

Before laws gave baboons a protected status, the troublemakers were killed by homeowners and farmers. By 2010, two dozen full-time "baboon monitors" were employed to protect the animals and shoo them away from residential areas. The monitors are doing their best to put an end to all this monkey business.

A weasel-like critter disrupted a professional soccer match by running onto the field and showing off some pretty good moves while players and grounds crew chased after it. Before it was caught, the animal left quite an impression — teeth marks on one of the players.

The Swiss League match between FC Thun and Zurich in 2013 was just getting underway when a wild pine marten — a cute but unpredictable woodland animal — made its entrance onto the pitch. The crowd laughed as it scurried about, dodging all those who tried to capture it.

FC Thun's goalkeeper, Guillaume Faivre, shooed the marten toward an exit. The rascal then ran up into the stands, scurrying past the feet of screaming fans who wanted no part of it. Not content to terrorize spectators, the marten reversed course and sprinted down the stadium steps and back onto the field behind the goal.

The animal tried to dart past Zurich defender Loris Benito, but the defensive wiz was too quick with his hands and grabbed it. That wasn't a good idea. What Benito failed to realize was that martens have razor-sharp teeth and a bad attitude, especially when being pursued.

So the marten did what any marten would do in such a situation: It bit Benito on the hand. The player let out a howl and dropped the critter . . . and the chase was on again.

This time, Zurich goalkeeper Davide Da Costa, who was wearing his soccer gloves, did what any goalie would do in such a situation: He blocked it. Then he snared the squirrely animal and was able to hold on to it because its teeth couldn't penetrate his gloves. Minutes later, the marten was removed from the stadium and released into the wild.

After the game, which Zurich won 4–0, Benito admitted that it was a dumb idea to have picked up the marten with his bare hands. "I was probably a little foolish," Benito told reporters. "You don't know what sort of disease it might be carrying. It [the bite] was painful. But I wanted to play the match, and now I simply trust my immune system."

CHOWHOUNDS

"MY DOG ATE MY HOMEWORK"

Reggie the dog had a hunger for learning, so he ate his teenage owner's science project — a large candy-covered volcano that took hours to make.

That was bad enough. Even worse, when he ate the volcano, he also swallowed more than 50 straight pins that were used in its construction, and he ended up undergoing emergency surgery.

For her eighth grade science class in 2013, Payton Moody, 13, of Englewood, Colorado, thought it would be interesting to make a replica of the Mt. Haleakalā volcano in Maui, Hawaii, out of various kinds of candy.

She pinned M&Ms and other sweet treats to a large piece of foam that formed the basic shape of the volcano.

"She had chocolate as the mountain and used Twizzlers for lava coming out, with blue M&Ms for water," Payton's mother, Kara, told GoodMorningAmerica.com. "She used the pins, because I didn't want the hot-glue gun around her younger brother."

Payton had slaved over the project and was looking forward to presenting it in class. "I woke up one morning and I came down to my desk, and the volcano was just all over the floor," Payton told KCNC-TV. She quickly figured out that Reggie — the family's two-year-old yellow Labrador retriever — had knocked the mock volcano off her desk and eaten it.

The pooch was lying on the floor, whining in agony. Not only had he consumed large amounts of chocolate, which is toxic to dogs, but he had scarfed down all the pins that held the candy together.

Reggie's family rushed him to the hospital, where X-rays showed the pins were in his stomach. Most of them were removed through his throat by a veterinarian who used an endoscope. Then a vet surgically removed the remaining five from his belly. Reggie stayed at the animal clinic for two days and made a fast recovery.

Payton found out that the classic "my dog ate my homework" excuse didn't work, even though it was true. She still had to redo the whole project. The second time, however, she made the candy-covered volcano without straight pins.

As for Reggie, "He didn't learn his lesson at all," Kara told GoodMorningAmerica.com. "[Payton] remade it with the hot-glue gun so there'd be no pins, and he still went after it."

At least Payton's second try was worth it. She received an A.

FUNNY MONEY

Sundance was a money-hungry golden retriever — literally. He ate five $100 bills.

The 12-year-old family dog put the money where his mouth is while accompanying his owner, Wayne Klinkel, of Helena, Montana, on a road trip to Denver, Colorado, over the Christmas holidays in 2012. Along the way, Klinkel and his wife had stopped at a restaurant for dinner and left Sundance in their locked vehicle.

Klinkel also had left five $100 bills and a $1 bill in the car's cubbyhole, which, in retrospect, probably wasn't a good idea, given Sundance's fondness over the years for eating anything within his reach.

When the couple returned about 45 minutes later, they saw the $1 dollar bill lying on the driver's seat and a half of a $100 bill next to it. The rest of the money was gone. Because the doors were still locked, it was pretty obvious to Klinkel where the remaining bills were — in the dog's stomach.

Knowing that paper money wouldn't fully digest, Klinkel followed Sundance whenever the dog went outside to take care of business. Donning rubber gloves, Klinkel sifted through the poop and was able to retrieve small remnants of the missing money. He was hoping that if he could piece together at least 51 percent of each bill that showed the complete serial number, he could get the U.S. Department of the Treasury to replace the chewed-up $500.

He told the *Helena Independent Record* that he thoroughly washed all the pieces, soaking them for about a week in a cleaning solution. Then he drained and rinsed the pieces, using a screen made for panning for sapphires, and set them out to dry. Next, he began the difficult task of painstakingly trying to put them back together much like a jigsaw puzzle — only it was a lot less fun.

Amazingly, he was able to reconstruct enough of the remnants to make more than half of each bill. He taped the pieces to form each torn-up bill, which was put in its own individual plastic bag. Then Klinkel sent the pieced-together money off to the federal Treasury, with a note explaining what happened, in the hopes the department would send him $500 in return.

Five months later, he received a check from the federal government for $500. On the bottom of the check, it said, MUT. CURR REFUND, which is government lingo for "mutilated currency refund."

"I gave Sundance a pat, showed it to him, and told him not to eat it," Klinkel told the newspaper. The owner wasted no time in depositing the check at his bank because he didn't dare leave it anywhere near Sundance.

After the story about Sundance's appetite for money went viral, Klinkel heard from other dog owners who had similar tales. He exchanged e-mails with a woman whose dog figured out how to open the zipper on her purse and then ate several $20 bills. "She never did recover her money," he said.

Now when Klinkel travels, he locks his money in the glove compartment.

Klinkel said he has forgiven his dog. "Sundance may have eaten my money, but what he took, he gives back in unconditional love," he said. Then with a laugh, he added, "It all comes out in the end."

DIAMONDS IN THE RUFF

Dogs can have expensive tastes. In at least two cases, pooches have eaten diamonds in jewelry stores.

Soli the golden retriever swallowed a $20,000 three-carat diamond at a store in Rockville, Maryland, in 2010.

George Kaufmann, co-owner of Robert Bernard Jewelers, was examining the expensive dazzler that had been brought in by a diamond dealer. Sitting nearby was Soli, a friendly six-year-old dog who often hung out at the store and greeted customers.

Somehow, the precious stone fell on the floor, so Kaufmann and the dealer began searching for the diamond, but couldn't find it. Realizing that it had dropped close to Soli, Kaufmann decided to check out the dog. "When I looked in Soli's mouth, there was the diamond," Kaufmann told PeoplePets.com. "In a flash, he swallowed it, and there was nothing we could do."

The dealer may have been a bit taken aback, but Soli didn't mind that he had swallowed a valuable treat.

Trying to remain calm, Kaufmann decided to let nature take its course, even though it meant that he had to collect and gather the dog's poop for the next few days. On the third day, there was a glimmer of hope because the jeweler saw something sparkle when Soli did his business. "The diamond finally appeared . . . fully intact and fine," he said.

A year later, the mascot of a jewelry store in Albany, Georgia, swallowed two diamonds totaling $10,000.

A lapdog named Honey Bun liked to greet customers of John Ross Jewelers. But the store's four-legged asset became a liability one memorable day in 2011. Owner Chuck Roberts was at his work desk in the back of the store. On the desk were four small plastic bags of loose diamonds, each about a carat, that he planned to set in earrings. Honey Bun was sprawled on the floor by his side.

Roberts went to the front of the store to wait on a customer who just walked in. When Roberts returned to the back, he noticed there were only three bags of diamonds lying on his desk. The fourth was on the floor — empty.

"I looked all over, and there weren't any diamonds, so immediately I knew Honey Bun had eaten them," Roberts told WALB-TV. The owner said that when he had left the chair, Honey Bun had quietly jumped from the floor to the chair and then onto the desk, where he indulged in his pricey two-diamond snack.

The precious stones didn't stay in the dog for long. He passed them and an earring backing the next afternoon.

Fortunately for Honey Bun, his owner wasn't angry at him. "I haven't scolded him to this day, and I won't," Roberts said. But now when the owner leaves his desk, he makes sure his chair is pulled way out.

PLAYING BY EAR

Kandii the puppy loved her owner's earrings so much that she snatched one right off the woman's ear and ate it.

The four-month-old Yorkshire terrier cross was sitting on the lap of her owner Margaret Heptinstall, 68, of Ryhill, West Yorkshire, England, eyeballing the silver earrings that the widow was wearing. Suddenly, the puppy jumped up, seized the earring from the woman's left lobe, and swallowed it.

"Kandii was so fast," Heptinstall told the *Wakefield Express*. "I knew straight away what she'd done, and I knew it wasn't good. I rang the vet, who told me to bring her straight in."

She rushed her dog to the animal clinic, where X-rays revealed that the earring was lodged in the puppy's stomach. "The earring was too big to pass through the puppy, and it also had a sharp spike on it that would have perforated her gut, so we had to open her stomach to remove the earring," Heptinstall told the newspaper.

The operation cost $1,300 to take out the earring, part of an inexpensive pair that she had bought in Greece during a vacation years earlier. But Heptinstall didn't care about the cost. She just wanted her puppy safe from any complications caused by the dog's fascination with jewelry.

Veterinarian Louise Mallinson told the newspaper that Kandii could have died if her owner had not acted as quickly as she did. "This was fairly major surgery due to the complications that could arise, but Kandii made a full recovery," she said.

Heptinstall, a grandmother of six, said, "When the earring was returned, it was all shiny and clean. But I am not going to wear them around Kandii for fear she will eat them again. I am sticking to old-fashioned ones that have a better fastening. But I will keep the earrings as a reminder."

GOBBLEDY-YUCK!

Louie, a large, mixed-breed puppy, wanted what the toddler in his human family had. So, when no one was looking, the dog sneaked into the tot's bedroom and selected a new diaper, a tube of diaper-rash cream, a bottle of baby lotion, and a children's book — and ate them all.

Weighing in at more than 60 pounds at the age of six months, Louie always acted as though he was starving by the way he wolfed down anything put in front of him — whether it was food or not. Knowing how Louie liked to snack on anything, the Stephen Cross family, of Louisville, Kentucky, was usually quite diligent about keeping the dog from swallowing things that weren't edible. Whenever the Cross family left the house for any length of time, they would close their bedroom doors to prevent Louie from chewing up or eating things that could harm him.

Unfortunately, the Cross's housekeeper wasn't aware of the family's policy. One day in 2013, she unintentionally left the door open to the bedroom of the Cross's two-year-old son. Louie noticed the door wasn't closed, so he went inside the toddler's room and began his bizarre feast.

"With the door left open, Louie went in and must have started nosing around next to my son's changing table," Cross said in a Veterinary Pet Insurance Co. (VPI) press release. "By the time my wife got home, Louie had eaten an entire tube of diaper-rash cream, a bottle of baby body lotion, a size-six diaper, and a book."

Because these are things that are hard to swallow, Louie began vomiting and was taken to the animal hospital, where X-rays were taken of the dog's stomach and intestines. Fortunately, Louie had already thrown up the items he had eaten and was beginning to recover from his weird meal.

"The veterinarian told us how lucky we were that surgery wasn't required to remove any remaining foreign objects," said Cross.

For being treated for ingesting objects from a toddler's bedroom, Louie earned VPI's title of "Most Unusual Claim of the Month" for August 2013.

Since the episode, the family has been even more vigilant about preventing Louie from chewing or eating harmful items around the house. Said Cross, "I was always worried that Louie would chew up rugs or sheets, but I never thought he would swallow our son's items."

Roscoe, a three-year-old standard poodle, can relate to Louie. The dog ate two plastic baby bottles and a wet diaper in 2009.

"We came home from shopping one afternoon to find chewed-up bits of plastic and pieces of diaper all over the house," Jamie Springer, of Great Falls, Montana, said in a VPI press release. "Roscoe is huge — about 93 pounds — so it wasn't exactly a challenge for him to pull the bottles out of the sink, but we're still not exactly sure how he got the diaper. We have a trash can for diapers, and the rotating lid is designed to seal the diapers off in a trash bag. Sometimes, if it gets too full, a used diaper will pop out when you turn the lid. That must have been what happened."

Roscoe seemed fine at first. But then he lost his appetite and began coughing and vomiting, so Springer brought him to the veterinarian. An X-ray revealed severe irritation in Roscoe's stomach, but there were no outstanding pieces of plastic or diaper in his intestines. The vet prescribed an antibiotic and some medication to soothe Roscoe's upset tummy. A few days later, the poodle started showing signs of improvement.

"We thought we were being careful by putting the bottles underneath a metal cover in the sink and using a separate trash can for the diapers, but we underestimated Roscoe's determination," said Springer. "A lot of the baby's items have a strong smell, and I think Roscoe likes the smell. You can't leave anything lying around or out in the open with a dog in the house."

COUNTER CRUISER

Cali the golden retriever turned into a pig when she gobbled down what would have been a family's main course — nearly five pounds of raw meat that had been marinating in the kitchen.

Her owner, John Young, of Rocklin, California, wanted to prepare a special meal for the family. So early one day in 2013, Young took out a large, uncooked London broil roast from the refrigerator, seasoned it, put it in a baking dish, and coated it with a marinade. Everyone was looking forward to enjoying a scrumptious dinner.

Apparently, so was Cali, who was watching the preparation with keen interest.

Knowing how much the dog loves to eat meat, Young wanted to prevent Cali from attempting to snatch a bite, so he placed the London broil in the middle of the kitchen island. Alongside the roast, he also put a bag containing a loaf of French bread.

Cali played it cool and pretended to ignore the marinating meat, although her nose kept twitching at the aroma. This was a rare occasion for her.

Later that afternoon, shortly before he planned to cook the meat, Young left to pick up his children from softball practice. He returned a few minutes later to discover that the family would not be enjoying any London broil for dinner, because there wasn't any. Cali the counter cruiser had eaten the entire roast.

"I made a concerted effort to place the dish in the middle of the island in our kitchen, so it would be out of the reach of our little scavenger," Young said in a statement released by VPI. "When I returned home five minutes later, the first thing I saw was the bread bag on the kitchen floor and Cali lying by the couch with 'that look' in her eyes. I thought she had just eaten the bread, until I looked at the island and saw the dish sitting on the edge of the counter void of almost five pounds of meat."

No matter how delicious the roast was for Cali, consuming that much London broil led to tummy turmoil. Fearing she might get seriously ill, Young took her to the animal hospital, where the veterinarian took X-rays and induced her to throw up. After a couple of hours at the hospital, Cali was sent home and put on a strict diet for several days.

Young said he had previously bought pet insurance, because Cali "has a healthy curiosity for getting into things she shouldn't." The distress from Cali's eating binge was named VPI's "Most Unusual Claim of the Month" for November 2013.

COOKIE MONSTER

During the 2010 holidays, when no one was around, Gus the Labrador retriever snacked on Christmas cookies meant for guests of his human family. He didn't eat just one or two cookies . . . or even ten or twenty, for that matter. No, he ate trays of the holiday treats — a whopping five pounds' worth.

"My wife and I had some guests staying with us from out of town over Christmas," Gus's owner, Ken Boll, of Cottage Grove, Wisconsin, explained in a VPI press release. "We had trays of cookies and fudge on the counter for them to enjoy, and we just kept replenishing everything throughout the weekend, so the trays were always full."

Boll wasn't concerned about his two-year-old dog eating the cookies, because Gus hadn't shown much interest in the treats. Besides, the various trays and tins were covered with lids or plastic wrap. So the cookies were left on the counter while Boll, his wife, and friends attended a Green Bay Packers football game.

The people were looking forward to munching on the cookies upon their return later that night. But when they went into the kitchen, the treats were gone — every one of them. "And there's Gus standing in the kitchen, wagging his tail, happy as can be," said Boll.

Gus managed to reach and consume not only every cookie on the counter, but also a plate of fudge and the plastic wrap that had been covering the fudge. He had even started chewing on a metal cookie tin. "He left the chocolate-covered blueberries," Boll said. "He must not have liked those."

Uncertain of how much of the chocolate in the cookies and fudge could seriously harm Gus, Boll took his dog for a late-night visit to an emergency animal hospital. The veterinarian weighed Gus before and after inducing vomiting to determine the amount of holiday snacks that had been gobbled up. "It was five pounds," Boll said. "The veterinarian got tubs of the stuff out of him." The over-eating dog had consumed one-eighth of his weight in cookies and fudge.

Boll said Gus never appeared to be in any discomfort before or after his visit to the veterinarian and went on to enjoy the holidays without further mischief. However, Gus did inspire Boll and his wife to make a New Year's resolution: "The next time you leave the house, make sure that everything is out of Gus's reach."

ABOUT THE AUTHOR

Allan Zullo is the author of more than one hundred nonfiction books on subjects ranging from sports and the supernatural to history and animals.

He has written the bestselling *Haunted Kids* series, published by Scholastic, which is filled with chilling stories based on, or inspired by, documented cases from the files of ghost hunters. Allan also has introduced Scholastic readers to the *Ten True Tales* series, about people who have met the challenges of dangerous, sometimes life-threatening, situations. He is the author of such animal books as *Bad Pets Save Christmas*, *Bad Pets on the Loose!*, *Bad Pets: True Tales of Misbehaving Animals*, *Miracle Pets: True Tales of Courage and Survival*, *The Dog Who Saved Christmas and Other True Animal Tales*, *Incredible Dogs and Their Incredible Tales*, *True Tales of Animal Heroes*, and *Surviving Sharks and Other Dangerous Creatures*.

Allan, the father of two grown daughters and the grandfather of five, lives with his wife, Kathryn, near Asheville, North Carolina. To learn more about the author, visit his web site at www.allanzullo.com.